Second 1ˢᵗ Step .....

... a search for answers after a tragedy

Reggie M. Colomb

regepett@yahoo.com

Scripture quotations are taken from the Additional Scripture quotations are taken from the *New King James Life Application Study Bible*, Copyright © 1960 by Tyndale House Publishers.

Edited by and Special Appreciation to:
Angie Harris & Marilyn Johnson

Layout/ Design: Kathy Bentz in collaboration with Reliance Media

Published by: RMCLifePub, Inc.

Printed and Co-Published by: NewBookPublishing.com

FIRST EDITION

ISBN: 978-1-936989-76-8

Library of Congress Control Number: 2012944234

Printed in the United States of America

Reliance
Media

Dedication

*This book happened by the grace of God
through the blessings of love from
my best friend, partner, wife
and mother of our children.*

Irene Godzik Colomb

May this book touch you …..

….. as a *reminder* your life can **drastically change** in a matter of seconds.

….. by *realizing* **all you have** at this moment, until you no longer have it.

….. with a *perspective* of **why** bad things happen.

….. through an *awareness* no matter how you look at yourself **another viewpoint** is always in play.

….. as *today's experience and challenges* will **strengthen you** tomorrow.

….. when *they say* you can't – **belief and desire** will lead you otherwise.

….. to *appreciate* the strength of **family love.**

….. with an *understanding* of **miracles**, know they are real and await you.

….. to *realize* yesterday is gone and your perceived mistakes or shortcomings can be **released.**

….. appreciating a *presence* in your life is forever **waiting** for you.

Reggie M. Colomb, PGA

Thank You .....   for taking your precious time to read this book.

The experiences you will be reading of can happen to anyone at any time and this I learned the hard way – by being primarily caught up in my own world so much that when a life-changing experience hit I was much less prepared than I could have been. My hope is as you travel the journey of this book you grab on to its messages and really peer at yourself from the outside looking in. If you are at total peace at this moment, consider journaling the elements contributing to your comfort. If you are feeling unsettled or discouraged, view this time as a time work is going on deep inside of you – a time of tremendous growth and re-building. Picture what your house is going to look like once the renovations are complete!

Wherever you are at this moment in your personal self, meaning your inner-being of mind and heart, a purpose of this writing is to be thought-provoking from a friend's standpoint. I ask you to consider with deeper appreciation just how precious life is and encourage you to take the time to appreciate even the most minute detail, seemingly insignificant – as purposeful, if not for now but for later.

As you see how a life was altered, please understand I am not a victim. Yes, there are few days that go by that I do not think about all that I deeply miss. As these moments hit, the warm enjoyable thoughts of having nearly 30 years with my precious wife keep the light of being blessed burning deeper than the dark side of absence. Being able to understand and live this approach takes time and work. Most importantly it took the desperate need for a change. They say changing is not easy, and I agree; however, change is needed to fulfill a purpose and one we may not even know at the time! But it is real and is driven by a purpose. For me that purpose was to fulfill another calling for my life. If the word victim is real perhaps the true victims in this story are the children and grandchildren whose time was cut short or did not physically exist with a true Angel!

It was difficult to think a tragedy was needed for me to get it. The hard fact for me is this becomes clearer each day that passes. In looking back over my life **a challenge to explore deeper** for a different meaning of my life's purpose was definitely very real. Searching for the answer of "why" led me to understand I had to pass through the tunnels, cross the bridges and walk the links that I did because that is what shaped me to be an instrument for someone else to grasp.

Touching the bottom of my life through a terrible loss, extreme emotional and physical pain, seeing my children hurt with me unable to help them as I had before, and in a place of not knowing where tomorrow will be, made me realize **the truest of facts** – that **I am not alone and never was!**

Again, this book is about maturity, realizing how living a life of taking loved ones for granted and self-centeredness is a race that will run its course until the day **that it is time to grow up!**

Growing up is my experience to define aspects of my life and is contrary, in nature.   Real growing up is my turning over to the one who **designed the plan for my life, my pursuit to determine this plan, grasp it fully, and my knowing I am still loved, unconditionally, even when I fall short of fulfilling this plan.** Maturing is **after falling short –** get up, wipe myself off and get back to it!

Medical journey .....

Intensive Care .....

As previously stated, this auto accident occurred six miles west of New Bern, North Carolina. The responding medical team from New Bern agreed it most appropriate to transport me, via med copter, to the Pitt Memorial Medical Center in Greenville, the most medically equipped hospital in the area to provide me care. Since that time the New Bern Medical Center has enhanced its facility's capacity to be more prepared to address similar intensive medical situations.

Initially, while I was in a coma and clinging to life by a mere thread, the hospital's medical team worked diligently to give me every opportunity to survive. Jennifer was also transported to this same facility as she suffered from a concussion, muscle pulls and a forehead contusion. Irene's body was taken to the New Bern Hospital. Janelle, at the tender age of 14, was so kindly cared for by North Carolina State Troopers from New Bern to Greenville. Special friends Phil Panzarella and Lorraine DiJoseph, club associates from where I worked, also reacted upon hearing of the accident to comfort and care for Janelle, physically alone for a short time, as her world was so suddenly shaken. Heather Staton, my future daughter in law, and her mom Becky, living near Charlotte, traveled to Pinehurst to pick up Chris, who was playing in a college golf tournament and received the call of the accident just prior to his teeing off for the event. Once together in New

Bern, our three precious children were cast into the doldrums of facing a life challenge that just hours before were circumstances one would only think of by hearing a news report from some other community and certainly involving a family other than ours. I cannot imagine the state of their young minds and spirits, individually and collectively, at such a horrific time.

In the intensive care unit I laid in a comatose state while the world's minutes, days and weeks passed by. Daily, "our kids" made the trek back and forth from Morehead City to love, see and support me. I was in the coma for a number of weeks. In discussion with medical professionals I later learned the state of a coma, like sleep, can be varying depths. One doctor suggested the "deep coma" was the initial period, while coma conditions existed for nearly twice that amount of time. Whatever the perspective, I have shared my resting condition with various interested people and will summarize the experience to be a period I would classify as constant thought – a long standing dream. Some details I recall vividly while others are less apparent. Clearly, I remember Chris telling me Irene had passed. He and others obviously were unaware of my experience of seeing her cross over as you will read in pages that follow. During that time Jennifer made the statement, "Daddy, don't you worry Janelle is being well cared for." I also have a clear recollection of dreams involving golf and country club operations, my profession for nearly 30 years.

The initial hurt to our baby …..

Jen was also medevac'd to Pitt Memorial as she had a concussion and head laceration. Janelle was first taken to the New Bern Hospital, the same place Irene's body was taken. I cannot imagine the state of Janelle's mind – the fear of the unknown. Chris was in Pinehurst readying to tee off for a college golf tournament when his cell phone went off in his golf bag. Upon hearing of the accident, he frantically called hospitals and law enforcement in an attempt to find out what had happened. The information he received was vague. Heather and her mom, Becky Staton, drove toward Pinehurst to meet Chris and bring him to us.

As previously stated, Janelle was transported by the North Carolina State Police to Greenville where she was told by hospital staff, in the caring presence of Phil Panzarella and Lorraine DiJoseph, her mother had died. Again, I cannot imagine the pain of our youngest child as she was motherless from that point. Janelle went to Jen's room to be with her as Jen was told the same grim news. Jen asked of my situation and was told my fate appeared to be the same as their mom. As Chris arrived at the hospital, he, Jen and Janelle were told last rites would be given to me as they headed to intensive care area. With the loving support of Heather and Becky, they proceeded to see my beaten body.

Every time this situation is relived, my body shakes in chills and my head fills with tears of pain while thinking about the situation our precious children were confronted with. Over a couple of hours their lives were turned inside out with darkness of pain and anguish. Not only did they lose one parent, but it appeared both parents would no longer be in their lives! Jen recalls, "Dad, as I saw you laying there all I could think about was how you were always our fix-it guy. Any time we needed strength and the word to drive on, despite the challenge, you gave the right words to us. And there you lay unconscious and without any sign of life. Pain can't describe what I know we all felt. We just held each other as we all said – Dad, you have to make it!"

My body was situated on an oscillating bed. I was filled with saline to protect my vital organs. My feet and legs were placed in support boots. Jen described my body as, "Dad, you were completely swollen and blown up. You looked like a body that I had seen in pictures of a person who had drowned and was under water for an extended period of time. It's almost indescribable. Your eyelids were so swollen they covered the area of your eye sockets. Your ears were huge and completely distorted your blown up head. With your mouth open we could see your teeth were totally shattered. Your body was connected to total life support. Heck, dad, you were alive and at that point what you looked like didn't matter a bit."

The first few days were touch and go as the Pitt Memorial staff worked diligently to keep me alive. Our kids stayed in the waiting room, being given a limited amount of time to visit me every two hours. Jen recalls, "The staff was really supportive and kind about letting us stay with you beyond the normally allotted time." Jen continues, "we all talked about how this was just a bad dream that needed to come to an end. In reflection, it is amazing how looking back on those days the true meaning of life is put into perspective."

Community good-bye …..

A Catholic mass in honor of Irene was said at St. Egbert's Catholic Church in Morehead City. Jen tells, "The support in the Morehead area was incredible. There were so many people the front lawn was crowded as the church was jam packed. The thing I remember most about the church was the number of kids – many of mom's previous or current students from Newport Elementary School, who at that time that were sobbing and calling for Mrs. Colomb to come back. That was really painful to hear! Family members came down from the northeast. Aunt Darlene and Uncle Chris, Aunt Stasia and Uncle Ed, and so many others were there. My friends; Jessica Pack, Ben Chavis, Cindy Lepore and Cathy Boothe, along with Chris' buddies; William Monts with Doug Kearse and Janelle's friends Anna Onorato and Khara Kowalski, all came to Morehead for comfort. Club members and staff stepped up to an unbelievable level as did my fellow employees at Enterprise. Ruth and Gary Zurn, neighbors in Brandywine Bay, coordinated an amazing meal and gift card program that meant so much. The outpour of people who wanted to be here but couldn't was amazing and to use your term – tremendously heartwarming and unforgettable."

Nearly a month passed from the day of the accident to the day the kids went to Vermont for the final rites to Irene. Stasia and Ed Ogorzalek, Irene's sister and her husband, worked diligently with the church and funeral service to delay the funeral as long as possible. Jen states, "We didn't know if you were going to make it and thought it best to do it all once, if that was going to happen.

So, we asked for the longest delay possible and kept praying for you to come out of the coma."

"The turnout to honor mom was incredible. As I think back, the love and support from everyone in Rutland, Vermont and that area was incredible. The number of people that said prayers never seemed endless. "

Back from the coma .....

On the day I became more aware of the world around me, I woke with Phil standing next to my bed, in tears, sharing deep eye contact and firmly holding my arm. Phil and "the kids" agreed he would stay with me as Irene's last rites and burial took place in Rutland,
 Vermont, a community where she and I had grown up, met and married. A Catholic Mass was said at Immaculate Heart of Mary Church, the same place Irene and I exchanged wedding vows 27 years earlier.

It was during this trip Jen received a phone call from Phil telling her I had come out of the deep coma. Later, Jen told me this news was certainly bittersweet, though all were in agreement it was God's way of my joining our children as they bid farewell to their mom. In Jen's loving words she said, "Daddy, you know through the love you and mom shared, the Lord made sure we were together as a family to say good-bye to mom and she is smiling with that in mind."

As the kids returned, seeing them for the first time was a moment like few others. Their hugs contained an energy I remember to this day. I remain so proud of the strength they demonstrated in my presence. Although they were hurting to a level I could not imagine, the bond they displayed is part of the greatest moments of my life. "We done good" was our precious statement Irene and I shared of the kids as we commented to each other following one of their accomplishments through the eyes of proud parents. This statement is a bit ironic as Irene, a teacher, was very articulate in her speech and writing, but it was our own affirmation.

Did he say what I thought he said?

A couple more weeks passed. Jen, Chris, Janelle and Heather continued visiting and sitting with me. I cannot imagine the state of their minds; perhaps this information will be conveyed in a future writing. At that point there was nothing I could do as a tube did my breathing for me and my body did what bodies do in that state. Medical records reflect minimal changes except my catching pneumonia, causing another storm the kids withstood. That was the third time these young lives faced the possibility of losing both parents in two months' time. Later, during a therapy session, I learned just how strong our three precious creations were! As you review the profiles of each, please join me in thanking God for His presence in their lives! When challenged by future physical therapy sessions — Jen, Chris and Janelle will never know how much their love during this tremendously dark time in their lives challenged me to move on!

One morning Jen had just finished rubbing my head when she stepped out of the room, then came back to see the doctor standing at the head of my bed. He said chilling words, "you need to be prepared to understand your dad is not going to walk, will have limited upper body mobility and his overall body functions appear to be at a minimum." Jennifer, shaking and eyes filled with tears, asked him to repeat his words. He made the same statement and I cannot imagine what this sounded like to her. Wasn't the immediate past enough bad news for these kids?

So badly, I just wanted to be dad by jumping out of bed, to grab Jen and hold her in an attempt to protect my firstborn from more hurt. But, looking around, seeing all the apparatus connected to me knowing I could not feel a whole lot, made my wish seem impossible. Furthermore, since I could not speak, frustration had to add to Jen's discomfort as our eyes met.

Within my mind I wanted to tell Jennifer that somehow, someway, she, Chris and Janelle had been through enough by having to bury their mom. Why couldn't those words just come out? Better yet, why couldn't I jump out of bed and realize I was just experiencing a horrific dream? I would tell Irene of the dream and she would assure me the thought came from a tear jerker she and I had watched the previous night!

And, of course, Irene would repeat her words of other movies we had watched together, "Rege, you act so tough, but I know before this movie ends you will be crying too." More often than not she was correct. However, this was no movie and the words spoken by the doctor were as real as the flow of tears streaming down Jen's hurting face.

Again, Jen looked at me and I could not respond. I realized I may be a burden to our children for the rest of my life. Jen came back up to my head and kissed me. As she did, I felt her tears drop on my face as she quickly wiped each, pretending to be unbroken.

Jen walked away and called Chris to tell him the update. She tried so hard to protect me from hearing these words. Wait, the protection thing was supposed to be **my** job!

Now I lay in bed, looked up to the ceiling and asked God if those words were really true. Was I really going to be unable to move? Within my mind I was yelling at God, asking Him what this was about and why didn't he let me just go at the accident? **It did not take me long to learn just how selfish and self-centered my words were.** I felt as though my head was swollen to the size of a beach ball and ringing!

All of a sudden I could feel warmth on my head as I closed my eyes to see **a bright light**. It reminded me of the light I observed around Irene as she passed. Was this my time? A voice told me to take a good look at myself as pictures of our family and children growing up moved through my head like a picture show. A voice then reminded me that I was a father and needed to handle the situation the best I could.

A calmness …..

It was at that point a sense of peace filled me. The supposed debilitating words meant very little, for I knew I was going to move regardless of the amount of effort it took – I would work to make our kids proud of their dad! How could I get this message to the kids and give them a sense of assurance that I was going to move and not be a burden to them? I will say I had a fleeting thought that perhaps that thought was a another "Regism" – a self-proclamation that fulfilled my ego and thought process. Somehow, though, I knew this wasn't the case. From that moment on – deep in my heart I never doubted I would be mobile in some capacity.

What I didn't know, though, was how I was going to convince my loved ones of my deepest assurance. **In reflection now, what I didn't think of then was - where did this feeling of assurance come from?** And, how was I so sure it was very real? **These answers would come from a place I never realized!**
The power of prayer! …..

Nearly every evening one of the kids stayed at the hospital with me. They made sure dad was not alone - selfless acts to their highest degree! Before going to sleep I thought back to our family prayer nights – re-living one after another while asking God for His mercy through the strength of helping me feel any part of my body.

Since I was a decent athlete as a kid, my thought was that if I could get my left, big toe moving other parts of my body would also awaken. After spending days compiled of many hours talking to this toe, I realized nothing seemed to be happening.

One of many cards sent to me by good friends Kevin and Carol Worley, from Columbia, South Carolina, contained words directing one to believe by talking to God, placing my petition before Him. As I listened to the words read by Chris, I realized I had not prayed in an honoring manner. Again, I was caught up in the thought things would happen by just my lips moving.

I began by thanking God for all my blessings. **Everything began and ended with Almighty God!** I didn't just say these words - **I believed them!**

One evening I fell asleep to be woken by a strange feeling. I looked down at my left foot, staring at it intently. All of a sudden my big, left toe moved up and down! And I could feel it! A couple days went by before I motioned to anyone about this movement, as other toes on my left foot started to move. Yes, I could think about moving my toes and they would move!

Exploring prayer …..

On the morning I made anyone aware of this movement my primary nurse Anne was working. She came to my bed, and Jen was standing there as I moved my eyes toward my left foot. Anne lifted the sheet as I winked at both these special ladies. I moved the big toe as Anne's eyes became as large as a half-dollar. A single tear rolled down Jen's face as her gorgeous smile lit up. Shortly, the same doctor that made the devastating statement to Jen came by to do his rounds. Anne brought him over to my bed and winked at me. Initially, I didn't move, then within a few seconds I waggled my left, big toe. The doctor said, "It's a spasm that would occur from time to time". At that point I continued to move as many toes as I could. The doctor became quiet as Jen came up to my head and gave me a kiss!

The next few days, when Chris, Heather and Janelle came to see me, the big news was the increasing movement, **by the Lord's hands**, of my toes! With their continued love, now massaging my feet and legs, increased feeling became more than a thought.

A special lady …..

My period in intensive care left me with a fond memory, a ray of sunlight in an otherwise dark time with the opportunity to meet a loving, caring nurse - Anne Chambers. Anne and I connected in a wonderful way. She seemed to know when I needed to see her special smile or receive an assuring held hand. Anne had a beautiful demeanor of being able to combine professionalism with gentleness and sensitivity. She made me feel like I was her special patient and she, my special nurse. When I attempted to communicate Anne took the time to concentrate on my lips, as I thought they were moving when actually, more than likely they were not. Through my eyes she read my messages while most often Anne conveyed my point to others. Jen, too, possessed this special ability. As I later discuss my life's spiritual development, this special relationship will be further expounded.   Anne also made sure to report my condition to Jen, Chris and Janelle. To me, her commitment is the clearest definition of a person who made a profession her vocation.

An unanticipated move .....

The hospital moved me to a unit called Intermediate Care. This area appeared to be a location for patients with uncertain futures or patients the medical staff is not quite sure where to place. The term, "intermediate", means transitional, provisional or conditional. To me my condition was not uncertain. I knew deep in my heart I was going to improve, I just needed to convince medical staff of my direction. Little did I know this challenge was going to be much more difficult than I anticipated. A voice inside of me kept saying I was not a cookie cutter patient with a checklist of points that determined my lot in life. During times of deeper thought I asked for the true meaning of this voice and from where it came? At this point I did not know, but I knew it spoke clearly to me. In the future this question would present itself time and again until I understood its purpose. How could I find its answer? I share my growth and answers to these questions as this book moves on.

On to a new area .....

After over a week of this intermediate experience, the hospital placed me in the rehabilitation unit. In this new setting my days were continued nursing care, as I remained connected by a breathing tube. My meals included closing my eyes and dreaming of the taste of grilled burger, my mom's stuffed peppers and some juicy, seedless watermelon. Upon opening my eyes, it was the same protein shake poured into my side through a tube. Jokingly, I likened my body to a car engine and requested an additional quart of oil. A good friend, nurse's assistant, Ellen Edmundson, responded by saying, "We will have to check to see if another quart is needed." These innocent exchanges built rapport, as the caring nurse respected the situation. We seemed to share an interest in attempting to keep the air light and the mood as positive as possible. My craving to taste a nice cold glass of water wouldn't leave me. I asked for a sip of water, my request for an ice cube met with Ellen's same loving response, "Reggie, as soon as we are able to remove the breathing tube you will be able to enjoy the water as well as that meal you keep requesting." Day after day passed while various practice breathing techniques challenged me, until one morning, a nurse told me my breathing device would be removed. Patient advocate James Barrett shook my hand and congratulated me as he heard the news! Unbelievable and as simple as it seems, the removal of this device meant a sense of freedom and movement in the right direction. Then came a heads-up that a swallowing check was scheduled. This test meant the possibility of eating real food. A little practice with awareness of how to handle the challenge, and my chances of passing this test was in right in front of me. It was clearly apparent there were people truly on my side, as many staff did everything each could do to assure my success. It was great to feel these two caring people rooting for me. The value of the caring words and touches of precious people like Anne, Ellen and Jim as I moved forward at Pitt Memorial, cannot be overstated.

To rehab ....

After a couple of weeks I was taken to the rehabilitation workout room. This was a bright room and what I remembered the most was the number of pictures on the walls of people sitting in wheelchairs. There were no pictures of people standing, walking or running. To me, this sent a message which did not sit real well with the little voice deep inside of me. Was I supposed to accept the wheel chair thing without a chance to improve? Therapists took me to the gym to attempt to do various tasks including lifting weights with my feet and arms, sitting without assistance and hand exercises. Because of my depleted strength, failure seemed inevitable; I couldn't complete even the smallest challenge. A picture of total dependence on others, regardless of what I wanted to believe, was certainly completely real at this time. This was an awful place to be!

As time went on it became apparent the therapists seemed to be as frustrated with me as I was in myself. My most satisfying time was going to an outside garden area with our kids while enjoying fresh air and natural beauty. Life's enjoyment became appreciation for fresh air and scent of a freshly, bloomed flower. Was this irony or an example to the circle of life within an individual being? In the garden I constantly thought about the burden I was becoming to Jen, Chris and Heather. They took turns bringing Janelle to spend time with me, driving between Morehead City, Wilmington and Greenville. My brothers David, Jeff and Mark, all in Vermont and Glens Falls, NY, also came to spend time with me. My oldest sister, Cheryl, living in Hialeah, FL, with whom I had fallen out of touch came to visit and shared her loving touch to my face. I wanted so badly be able say how much I appreciated her loving touch when I was a child. Special friends and club members, Hoover and Donna Taft, who lived in Greenville, visited me often and brought me home cooking. Other people associated with the Country Club of the Crystal Coast – Lorraine and John DiJoseph (Lorraine the club's office manager) and Phil Panzarella also visited me bringing words of encouragement and love. Lorraine told me friends' inquiries from Vermont to South Carolina, and those of club members, kept her busy as she established a daily update email program for people who constantly called the club. All the prayers and words of encouragement were more powerful than any of these people will ever know. These were the bright lights in the darkest of times.

Fitting what? .....

One morning a nurse came to my room and said I needed to get up early as I had a fitting appointment.

I asked why I needed to be fit for another body cast since a new one had been put on me just a few days before. She said these chilling words, "this is a fitting for your chair". At first this statement didn't register. After a few moments, though, I called and asked that she come to my room as I inquired if this meant what I thought it did. The nurse affirmed my sickening feel that this fitting was for my permanent way of life – a power wheelchair. My statement to the nurse was that the chair I was currently using would suffice until I walked. She did not respond and said it was time to get ready for my visitor. A short time later a gentleman came in and I made the same statement to him. He said that he was doing his job as directed by a doctor's work order. To this day, these are chilling statements to think about. Was this really my future life?

A few weeks passed while little changed in my physical life. I was unaware of what was going on inside my inner being. I enjoyed hearing words from television ministers Joel and Victoria Osteen, Jimmy and Karen Evans, Joyce Meyers, Bishop T.D. Jakes and Dr. Charles Stanley. As this book moves forward, you will realize the impact of these special messengers of God and their contributions to the future of my life.

One Wednesday, Jen showed up earlier than usual to see me. Her face was more drawn and certainly reflected concern at a deeper level. I asked Jen what was happening, and she said the staff had contacted her to let her know I was being discharged the following Friday because I was not cooperating with the hospital staff. What did this mean? I didn't like the wheelchair fitting thing; however, I had not been disrespectfully uncooperative. She went to a meeting and then came back to my room and said my inability to do the required exercises, instructed by the physical therapists, meant they really did know what to do with me.

I asked Jen where I was heading. She said she would speak to Chris and they would do the best they could to keep moving forward. That evening was one of the longest in my life. It hurt so deeply that my children had to deal with me and were disappointed I could not accomplish the rehab exercises. I cried all that evening. The next morning Joyce Meyers was speaking with a message about challenging times and how **"Christ is the true light"**. These words hit me square in the heart and continued to ring within me for days. The word **light** seemed to have an intense meaning. Later Jen came back after her day of work. Again, I cannot put into words the appreciation I have for Jen, Chris, Heather and Janelle for being patient and loving with their dad! Jen told me she and Chris had spent the evening contacting care facilities. She said the only place that had available space was the Sea Level Nursing Home located over an hour outside Morehead City. Jen explained that because of my young age, coupled with my care needs, the only facility near Morehead which could offer me care was this nursing home. Jen said I would be transported there on Friday and we would go on from there.

Heading out and meaningful words .....

Friday morning I was placed in an ambulance and made the four hour trek to Sea Level. Once there, the staff fulfilled Jen and Chris' request that I be placed in a single room. The staff was very kind as many stopped by and expressed condolences for the passing of Irene and mentioned how impressed each was with the meeting of Jen, Chris, Janelle and Heather. They promised to do all they could for me. Members of each shift came in to my room and provided me their own tour of the facility. The next day the kids all came and we took another tour of the facility. I will never forget the look in their eyes as they apologized for having to place me in a nursing home. Their hurt was tearing me up inside. But again, the love each showed me cannot be measured; I saw Irene's gentleness and caring in each of them. After the kids left for the evening at the end of the day I went to the chapel. One of the evening aids followed me and asked if they could assist in any way. I asked if she could place the bible on my lap and turn to **Psalm 23.** Recently, Joel Osteen referred to a verse in one of his television messages and its words stuck with me – **"My shepherd is Lord. I shall not be in want."** I kept reading these words over and over. For days I said these words along with constant prayers – **The Lord's Prayer.** Growing up as a Roman Catholic **The Lord's Prayer** is a staple. Saying these words was comforting as I remembered family time on Sunday evenings when we would all gather on our bed, pray together and share thoughts about the week ahead. These times, although gone, were a wonderfully fond memory of precious family time.

Daily, my mobility began with my being lifted like an engine being removed from an auto (using a hoyer lift) and placed in the wheelchair. I had no control over my body functions other than the ability to see, whisper and chew. My left side had little mobility, while I could move my right hand and lift my right arm to a point about chest high.

The first part of the next week began by going to the little workout room where the two therapists, Richard Smith and Andy Gardner, worked with me while providing constant positive reinforcement. By the end of the first week I had convinced Richard to let me go into the room so I could grab hand and limited leg weights. I promised jump roping and deep squats would be limited! By the end of the second week he strapped me on a standing board, which allowed me the chance to see the world from a vertical position for the first time since the accident. This exercise, although just seconds because the quick blood rush to my head would cause issues, was wonderful and motivated me more than they knew. While vertical, the words **"I shall not be in want"**, really hit me and rang in my head.

Life around a nursing home is not highly recommended from my standpoint. I can appreciate the need for the work these places do; however, there is no place like home. Since I was considerably younger by probably 20 years than the average resident, my life's perspective was a bit different. Daily bingo became a bit old for me. On the lighter side, the kids enjoyed hearing of my experience with one of the residents who decided walking around without clothing was to her liking. My room seemed to be a spot she enjoyed visiting! Since I was not mobile, my protection was to pretend to be sleeping – soundly, very soundly! All I can say about that is I'm sure this lady was lovely, say some 40-50 years prior! Anyway, no harm – no foul! To date, Jen continues to enjoy telling of that experience – and she laughs just as hard to this day as she did the first time I told her about my visiting friend!

To our home …..

My stay at Sea Level lasted nearly a month. The kids knew I was not happy and agreed to move me back home and provide as much care as they could with the assistance of home health care. Hospice coordinator Patti Schweis, a club member, scheduled their program to help us at home. Carolina Physical Therapy Clinic in Morehead City, with Roxanne Mannino, Deena Stern, Lisa Smelik, Jenny Hill and Karen McCormack, was a setting that introduced me to more intense therapy. Heather was considering nursing as a career and spoke with the therapists as she enlightened me of my current condition and shared their thoughts about my possible improvements. Lisa was my primary therapist when I first became a patient at the clinic. Along with Heather, Lisa played a key role in gaining access to New Hanover Medical Center (NHMC) Rehab, in Wilmington, North Carolina, where significant physical improvements took place. Deena then took over as my rehab coach and pushed me in a loving and determined way. Roxanne, a massage therapist, worked with me then and for a couple years following my discharge from the clinic's care. I believe Deena's pushes and Roxanne's work on my legs were key to my gaining improved blood flow and healing. Roxanne also became a special friend as she constantly shared positive, upbeat words of encouragement.

A new hospital …..

Heather received a phone call from NHMC that an opening existed as long as I could get to the hospital within the next 24 hours.

The way this whole situation was so detailed and precise **divine intervention** had to occur and could easily be classified as a minor miracle. My definition and appreciation for miracles is explored more in depth later in this text.

Once in New Hanover, I immediately became acquainted with a team of special people that will forever hold a place in my heart. Lead nurse Barbara Hargett Smith, primary physical therapist Amber Ponnett, occupational therapist Noa Alper, floor physician Dr. Xi (pronounced "Z"), my confidant, great friend, Dr. John Liquori, chief neurologist and the clinic's team leader, was the professional team which held my life in their hands. So many other wonderful professionals created a setting of unlimited blessings, including Rutland native, nurse Laurie Rose and nurse's assistant Eula Robinson. Freddy Simpson, most often my evening nurse, physical therapists Mike Stine and Dana Pastorek, worked with me on days Amber was away. Recreation therapist Sarah Bentley was great with her daily joking, and as time moved on we would work together to organize patient, team building activities. These are but a few of so many special people that truly were my teammates during this chapter of my life and my **Second 1st Step**.

During our initial meeting, Dr. Liquori asked me my goals. The words, "I plan on walking out of here" flowed, without thought, from my lips. In the next few days all these wonderful people, each in his own way, shared that the likelihood of my fulfilled goal was more than unlikely. However, each committed with sealing hugs, to contribute and accompany me on the way.

Therapy of any kind is a testing, grueling process. My experience and recommendations will be contained in future writings as this topic is so in-depth and challenges our deepest self. The dedicated people making therapy a vocation are magnificent, for the most committed become absorbed in every movement of their patient. The relationship between therapist and patient is as intimate and bonding as can exist. The special therapists told me a patient overcoming a challenge is the greatest rush they experience. As Amber reflects on the valuable moments, "Reggie, during our studies and clinical experience therapists try to make a difference in another person's injured self who otherwise often has minimal hope. We work to develop rapport and place ourselves in the patient's situation so each knows we are vested in their life. A patient's accomplishment is a family success. Future energy is drawn from previous efforts and the joy of being with a patient during his success." From a patient's standpoint the excitement of improvement is deeper when shared. One's family appreciates seeing the physical improvement and the very apparent outward patient respond, as well. The therapist's hug or handshake is a touch the patient will hold onto forever!

His work is continuing …..

As weeks and months passed my every moment was filled with purpose. A real sense of strength filled my mind and body. During weekday mornings I woke hearing the words of Joyce Meyers. On the weekend Joel and Victoria Osteen and Dr. Charles Stanley filled my room with spiritual blessings and prayer.

One message taught me the effectiveness of **praying with others, for others and not just for yourself.** The message said God is pleased by the generosity of praying for others.

Through my golf and country club experience I previously learned the importance of fresh, good air, often called karma. **To me – it's God's hands - the essence of belief filled with prayer!**

Each morning I woke early, did a quick jaunt down to the rehab gym then back up to our hospital wing - to visit other patients as a start to my day in prayer for my fellow "hotel guests"! The prayer for others was therapeutic and gave a sense of purpose and bonding. In testimony Judy Bates , a special lady who had suffered severe spinal injuries similar to mine, was told her mobility was going to be extremely limited. It was apparent as Judy showed improvement far beyond expectations that an energy had certainly touched her life. Judy and I became friends, and her two sons came by my room as they left each evening. We had great conversation as the boys shared the feelings of pain for what they saw their mom going through. We shared Bible verses and committed to believe a miracle was available for the asking. Judy's condition improved tremendously, as did the spirit of her sons. Seeing this was so motivating and strengthening! Also, serviceman Carl Traub, who had lost both his legs, miraculously learned to adjust to prostheses with strength.   Our friendship grew as we challenged each other to work as hard as we could. Carl was so motivating for me. Daily we shared prayers for other patients and worked to keep positive energy flowing throughout the gym.   Carl exuded excitement for the days ahead with his wife and two children. Since my discharge the opportunity to spend time with challenged patients like Judy and Carl, along with so many loving families, repeatedly demonstrates **praying has purpose!**

Periodically, "the patient team" showed appreciation for our caregivers by preparing lunch. These exercises gave all of us chances to put our physical abilities together and continued to contribute to the atmosphere of positive enthusiasm filled with belief of a brighter tomorrow! Coordinating these activities earned me the nickname "governor". It was really a specific message of Joel Osteen through the precious words of the Bible that prompted us to share our love without any expectation in return. The Lord's presence assisted different patients' ability to slice a tomato, butter bread for garlic toast, scoop sauce on manicotti, place table settings and fill pitchers with lemon water, etc., basic tasks for most people. However, in this world the efforts epitomized team work and just how powerful **UNITY with PURPOSE, in HIS NAME**, can be!

Highlighting some days …..

So often during rehabilitation, the Spirit reminded me of words and actions that were part of my successful golf instruction program. Experiences of 20 or more years ago, apparently of little significance other than to reinforce an instructional point at that time, were words with much greater impact later on in my life. I look at an energy well beyond me to know everything that has happened, the good and bad, has a purpose – its meaning may not show until later. Understanding a master plan has been designed for each life is so clearly stated by my four friends – Joyce, Victoria, Joel and Dr. Charles - during their messages. Whenever the question of "why?" entered my head, the precious words of these masterful carriers of the Lord's message kicked me back on line.

In further study, I read books outlining the natural maturation of children as they learn to walk. Recalling each of our children as they scuffled along the floor, learned to use their toes or bottoms to move, challenged coordination and strength enough to get to their knees, grabbed on to a couch edge and then worked themselves to their feet, all my exercises assumed a deeper meaning. If this was the process I needed to go through in order to walk – I would.

Pushing hospital rules – I'm sure .....

Many early mornings I slid from my bed to the wheelchair so I could sneak into the gym for a piece of equipment to work on my strength. Then back up to our floor and prayers with fellow patients. Then, the challenge to get back in bed while God knows the number of times I fell short during the attempt, ending up on the floor with lovely Eula Robinson helping me get back in bed like nothing happened. Should a hospital official read this book, please look on Eula's work as the hands of God leading her for assistance to share His work. It was the pressure of a highly persistent patient that Eula was tending to as she demonstrated the love of a most giving professional.

Amber cautiously outlined a working plan as we began to do exercises in order to return strength to my legs and hips. As we began it was all I could do to lift a rope tied to my foot, let alone lift with weights added. My weakened hands and arms then became the focal point, prior to the cautious removal of my upper body cast. Work to gain sitting balance on a rehab bench then followed. It was all I could do to lift a paper cup to enjoy a sip of juice. A simple task of brushing my teeth took at least 20 minutes. Squeezing the tube took tremendous effort as my arms were so weak, holding either up for more than a minute at a time, was another challenge. Both Amber and Noa showed tremendous patience, belief and support, especially during times when I broke down sobbing in tears. Any time my confidence shook these precious ladies lovingly wiped my tears, moved on with conversation as though nothing happened and kept moving forward without a break in the task at hand. Again, the blessings of angels continued to fill my life.

The whole rehab staff was supportive beyond belief and truly connected with my family and me. Over time the faces of Jen, Chris, Heather and Janelle appeared more relaxed as they witnessed even the slightest sign of my advancement. I fed on their positive energy with every challenge and felt as though they were with me with the final push of every exercise.

Still, the focus for me to walk was all-encompassing. The images of strolling around our neighborhood, Brandywine Bay, back in Morehead City, and walking into the new clubhouse at The Country Club of the Crystal Coast, were scenes I could really taste.

The challenges to my patience, a definite weakness of my earlier years, showed with every motion I tried to make. Surely, this was a designed exercise for my maturity by someone that knew me best. How many times was I told to be patient by my loving wife? Yet, while playing golf, the feel to strike at the right time to win a tournament and my ability to convey importance, the importance of patience to a lesson taker, was second nature. Later, my good friend Dr. Liquori often commented, "the challenges to your patience worked both for and against you."

One of the biggest challenges to my patience was the period of time leading to removal of my upper body cast. The first cast was placed on me in Pitt Memorial. With my body filled with fluid and my inability to eat meals of substance I continued to lose weight very quickly, causing the need for constant new casts. After being fit for the 16th cast, I lost track of the final total. By the time I checked in to New Hanover Rehab changing body casts was so frustrating. As the experience continued it reminded me of a past club member Rick Livingston. Rick, from back in my Mid Carolina Club management days, in South Carolina, brought laughs to many members, and me, as he said he was quitting golf nearly every time he played because he had played a poor round for him. Rick, a good player, usually scored between 74 and 77. Occasionally, as golf works, Rick was off his game and would balloon all the way up to 81 or 82, so he was giving the game up. During my recovery, I believe I had been fit close to 20 casts. Come to think of it, Rick may have said he was quitting many more times than my cast changed. The cast's purpose was to support my back and neck.

Use of the device seemed to have been important, although, it was tremendously uncomfortable and irritating. The day Dr. Liquori told me the body cast was being removed was so liberating I hosted a cranberry toasting party in my room! Hey, stay with me here – your preference may not be cranberry, but enjoy the meaning of the moment anyways! To me it was a milestone.

The chance to stand up despite total support of a standing frame, did so much for my psyche. It was even better these times than the first time Richard helped me with it at Sea Level. Imagine sitting in a chair or lying in a bed for nearly a year, looking at people's belly button areas. Because of the blood rush to the head thing, my times on the standing frames had to be carefully programmed, as did the duration of standing time doing so. The first time the kids walked in and saw me standing was precious beyond belief. We were able to look at each other standing face to face.

Time in the swimming pool and riding a stationary bike also increased as my breathing capacity improved. The ability to transfer myself from the wheelchair to the stationary bike was critical as I was able to expand my "homework – time before and after the workout area was open." Again, certainly outside the rules, but something I felt had to be done in order to become stronger and stronger. I worked really hard to discern the presence of staff in the area, for getting caught would more than likely threaten my continued residence. And I knew someone was watching over me so the chance of getting caught was somewhat guarded.

Since health insurance payments to facilities restricted the amount of work-out time I was getting, I knew my extra effort was needed. Also, to me, every moment my body laid dormant was time for it to revert to a stationary condition. For months rest was a majority of what I did, besides thinking and later praying, so now was my time to "make hay." When I was tired I knew my body would crash. But for that time – movement was the order of the day, as many moments within each day as possible.

Medically, I did not feel I could hurt myself any more than my body was already broken and twisted. Psychologically, my motivation to keep working was largely attributed to my kids for all they had gone through, along with the strength each demonstrated. I remained committed – those kids deserve a dad – not a burden! Spiritually, the words of my newfound God coaches also worked to keep me pumped up and on course. I made sure I didn't have time to feel down by filling my mind and heart with words of so many miracles stated in the Bible. Also, anytime I felt pain exercising, three thoughts came to my mind:

1. Thought of the pain **Jesus endured** as He carried the cross up Calvary before being crucified. **Can you imagine the pain of each spike being driven in his body?**
2. Imagine the pain **Jesus suffered** when the **crown of thorns** was placed on His head. **Did I force this crown deeper into His head by my continued sins?**
3. The words – pain is weakness leaving the body.

While pushing myself, if one thought didn't motivate me, another certainly did. My supposed pain was nothing compared to all that **the only true man** confronted.

Whatever it is that you are being faced with, and I can only imagine your hurt, please keep in mind a better day is ahead and together we will see it!

Again, God kept me alive for a purpose – it was time for me to prepare myself for its reason.

In late October I left the hospital. My checkout time was supposed to be at 9 a.m. At close to 11 I was moving around our floor like a caged animal, until finally the nurse came to get me. Once down on the main floor, sitting in a wheel chair, I turned a corner heading toward the hospital's entrance to see the rehab and medical staff lining the path to the door as I stood to my feet for a few assisted steps, with Amber and my children at my side, and headed out. At the door stood Dr. John Liquori, wearing a white dress shirt clearly drenched from his own tear drops. Standing across from Dr. Liquori was my new found friend, Judy Bates, who just a day before, stood on her own for the first time in months, all clapping and knowing we had taken a few steps some said would never be taken!

On the ride home for good –

When first settled into our handicap transport rental vehicle, Jen and I made eye contact when she looked in the mirror and asked if I was ready to head home. Our eyes were filled with tears as we shared a precious smile. Also in the vehicle was Jason Salter, Jen's husband at a later date.

The ride to my home was approximately 90 miles. It was nice to again see the world as we rode and not from a hospital window or riding along the road on a wheelchair. What a breath of fresh air!

As we became closer to Morehead City, my stomach started became very unsettled. I was going to be sleeping in our bedroom for the first time since the night before the accident became reality and hurt! As we pulled into our driveway I saw work my fellow employees from the CC of the Crystal Coast had done. What a nice gesture.

Entering my home through the garage led me into our family room, a place clearly apparent of Irene's touches, as golf memorabilia and family pictures filled the room. My emotions were mixed with the comfort of being home, but, a presence was clearly missing.

This room is below the home's main floor. I started to climb the four stairs, an exercise I had done numerous times during my recent rehab program. As I reached the kitchen at the top of the stairs my legs gave way and buckled. Thank goodness Jason was present, as he helped me to get into my wheelchair. We then went into my bedroom. At the door I had to grab my breath and say a prayer for strength as I transferred into my bed. Jen and Jason were so loving and kind as they made sure I was completely settled in. My first night's sleep was limited but I was reminded by a warm presence that filled the room.

Irene …..

"Mrs. Fucci, I cannot believe I just did what I did", were my words. Yvonne Fucci was the school secretary at Northwest Elementary School and my point of contact for the kids I have volunteered to spend time with as a basketball coach and "big brother". Yvonne and her husband Bob have been good friends since those days. Back then Yvonne and Bob consistently showed up to support me during my participation in golf events. Irene often stated, "It was Yvonne, Rege, that brought us together."

On that morning, standing by the entrance to the school was a young lady in a serious discussion with one of my boys "Big Nick". She looked so young I thought she was a student teacher. I asked her to step away, as I wanted to speak to her about the situation involving Nick. I introduced myself as Nick's coach and mentor to better select my time to speak up on behalf of the youngsters, especially before each gets into trouble.

Yvonne laughed saying, "Reggie, Irene Godzik is one of our teachers and is the lady I previously told you I wanted to introduce you to for a date. The other teachers thought you two would be perfect for each other." I guess my big mouth blew that. Yvonne continued laughing commenting she would speak to Miss Godzik, "to iron out the issue and make her aware of how much you love the kids."

The following weekend, my buddies Joe Davine, and Bill Merritt, and I decided to head out to the Wobbly II, a Rutland nightclub. Joe was to meet a girl who was bringing a couple of her friends with her. As we approached the table I immediately recognized one of the women as the same "Miss Godzik" I had so effectively made a jerk out of myself in front of just a few days earlier. When our eyes met, Irene made a cute comment, "My, it is the coach, ladies. Watch out how you speak to the boys at Northwest School or the coach will have a talk with you." Embarrassed, I acknowledged there was a need for me to defend a young man who was being excessively scolded by a teacher. The joking continued for a few minutes, or at least until I bought Irene Godzik a beverage.

That night ended early the next morning as we danced the night away and spent many hours talking about everything from Irene's interest in teaching to my enthusiasm for golf. We decided to go to a football game and then to a mutual friend's house party after I returned to her home to meet her parents. From the third weekend of October 1976, Rene and Rege become a couple. The following January I went to school at Jacksonville University, FL. The same February, Irene suffered a substantial loss, as her father passed away after a sudden heart attack. In February, 1978, I began an enlistment in the U.S. Air Force. We were married in July 1978.

Throughout 29 years of being together, we both grew into the strength of marriage of two best friends and life-long partners. We agreed one of our greatest blessings was our partnership and unity of two very different lives from unlike family experiences. We shared excitement to have two or three children. We agreed our parenting would be a partnership, speaking through one voice. Irene took the lead in each child through their initial 10-12 years while I led discussions as Jen, Chris and Janelle matured through their middle, high school and college years. Irene represented a calming effect within our house and was the tying knot holding our love together. When Irene was upset it was time to draw her a bath, place a bottle of wine with a new romance novel next to the tub and get out of the way. Most often that was just enough for Irene to settle back in to her peaceful self. People blessed to know Irene knew they had a solid, loving and true friend. Irene was a strong, committed woman who loved every one of her students (as an elementary teacher) and especially her family. In 1997 we were living in Irmo, SC when we heard a knock on the door. A postman handed Irene a book "Who's Who Among America's Teachers". In the book Irene's name was submitted by a student Irene taught back in 1983. The student reflected that Irene's love and belief in her gave her the strength to move on in spite of a difficult family situation. So often, prior to our move from Vermont, we would see a younger person who approached us to hug Irene and thank her for her kindness and caring as a teacher. I was so proud of Irene for all the lives she touched so deeply. Irene reflected balance of love and consistency for every person who ever knew her.

As a mother – the position Irene was most proud of, she loved its challenges. Irene loved to read to our children and often, even when Jen and Chris were at college returning for a break, we would talk about what each wanted to do as a family activity. Time and again voices would say, "Mom we want you to read to us. We'll make some popcorn and lay on your bed while you read to us." Irene's little face would light up every time she heard this request, and her reading reflected so much enthusiasm and emotion. Those moments were better than going to a movie. Also, that family time was simple, deeply warm and clearly signified the truest meaning of a mother's love! Irene said she enjoyed being my wife and partner. She was tremendously tolerant of a man whose self was out of balance. Irene appreciated the demands of being a country club manager and golf professional when the average work week was most often in excess of sixty hours, some weeks even more. Irene was supportive of the club as she came to the pro shop to set up displays and move inventory around. It is customary that the retail pro shop is owned by the professional. Irene had a natural retail eye and her touch was so apparent. My success with clubs was largely attributed to my family's support. Irene's presence during club functions provided a level of peace and comfort for me. Seldom did a day go by that Irene missed telling me how proud she was of me for all I did for club members. Her most precious words, "Reggie, the members will never know how much you give for their enjoyment and the club's success. I love you for this." I likened my commitment to Irene's for each of her students and I loved her for that!

Since this section is one of my final writings in this book, it is over five years since her cross over to be at the Father's Right Hand. Wherever heaven is, Irene is there next to her daddy, Frank Godzik! I wish I could remove the pain of Irene's passing from our children, but I know she is proud of the love each reflects and is part of their being as the natural chemistry passed through their mom!

Why building a relationship with God is important?

As my life has taken a drastic turn based on a most painful circumstance, the loss of the person I thought to be my lifelong mate, best friend, partner and mother of my children, there are at least two avenues I could choose to take; one – see myself as a victim, hold on to this position for the rest of my life and look to blame; or two – reflect on the opportunities of completely sharing me with a precious person, a lady in every essence of the word, a caring person who taught many so much and a woman who lovingly, completely embraced being a wife and mother. Irene often said how proud she was to be my wife and could not have imagined being blessed with any greater children than Jen, Chris and Janelle. "Our family is the essence of my life", often flowed from Irene's lips.

Through your reading to this point it is my hope you see the second choice has become my path. Please do understand I realize there will be difficult times ahead without this lovely person. There are certain triggers and moments that will bring back the darkness of the horrific moment when the sound of a tire blowing followed by the motion of our auto starting to roll over will return. Each time our children, their families and I will share time there will be an absence of a precious smile that means so much to each of us and our family unit as a whole. When such a time hits it is important for me, to remind myself of the opportunity to share so many precious moments with Irene before she crossed over to eternity. Such reflection is critical to moving forward.

To answer the question as to why God is important to me I reflect on the endless number of experiences that have shaped my life. Just having the opportunity to love and be loved at the level of our marriage was a gift shaped by a control and attention to detail well beyond me. I believe my Lord, God was just that source of energy and designed the blessing plan that led to our coming together. Our upbringing and interests were different just enough that our common pursuits formed the foundation that we grew to enjoy building upon. So many times Irene and I shared the perspective that through **faith** we were blessed with so much. Challenges to our marriage confronted us and led us to growth and increased closeness. And, when I look back on our relationship a number of good to great things that happened in our lives together, it is apparent these **blessings** also came from God. His presence in our home enabled us to mature individually, as a couple to one and as a family. The intricate birth of our three beautiful children was miraculous also indicating God's blessings to Irene and me.

Immediately after the passing of Irene and during my initial recovery I felt fear and uncertainty as I thought I was completely alone for the first time in many years. Although outwardly portraying confidence, my deepest self was scared to death, my physical and emotional conditions would not improve. As I opened my head and heart, finally admitting just how uncertain I was about my future, little signs came to me. I saw beauty in places that were previously unnoticed and felt more peace than I could have imagined. These conditions intrigued me and I learned through reading and listening to medical professionals, as well as a number of messengers of His word, my comfort was the presence of the Holy Spirit that filled me. As my knowledge grew I realized I was never alone. Fear and uncertainty gave way to a grown sense of peace and positive anticipation of what God had planned for the next chapter of my life.

The challenges that motivated me to share my journey also led me to search for deeper meaning and purpose. It is at this point I realize it is not for me to ask why but rather, how.

How can I thank God for the gifts of Irene, Jen, Chris and Janelle in my life? How can I thank God for the second chance to become more assured that I will enjoy eternity as well? How can I know and fulfill my life's new purpose? Throughout the remainder of this book I attempt to answer these questions.

Eternal peace …..

Time and again bright lights appear in my mind each time I am brought back to the moments at the scene of the accident. In spite of the circumstance, the experience will prove to be one of the most powerful moments of my life. The impact is so precious; my hands shake as I prepare to share the experience with you. My heart is filled with so much warmth as total peace fills me. May the words touch you in a way that inspires you to continued growth beyond even your imagination?

On highway 70, six miles west of New Bern, all of a sudden a loud pop occurred. The back, left tire of our vehicle blew out. The car began to twist from side to side. Then, the motion starting forward and the vehicle began to roll. After a quick "oh, shit", the moment went blank.

All of a sudden, I started to walk toward the vehicle to check on my ladies. Approaching the vehicle, Jen was still in her seatbelt with a little cut over her eye. This gash would later be significant. Janelle finished climbing through the window opposite her seat. She stood, arms folded saying, "my mommy is lying there and hurt". These trembling words would be earth-shattering. I passed Janelle and walked toward my loving wife's body, as she was laid on the side of the road. I lifted her lovely head and gave her a kiss. She did not respond. This was unusual, for we often spoke that even when one of us was asleep, the one of us sleeping would move in such a way to acknowledge the kiss. I then kissed my love a second time, again without response. My head turned to the left as I gazed into the sky filled with questions. All of a sudden a force pulled my attention to the sky. A bright light held me locked over my right shoulder while an incredible warmth and softness filled the space around us. Suddenly, Irene's face appeared with a smile that spread from ear to ear. She was more gorgeous than ever! Her eyes locked into to mine as faces of deceased loved ones began to encircle Irene's brilliance. The background looked like a cotton wall and enhanced the comfort of the whole setting. What was this about, although Irene's apparent peace and joy screamed out? With her being away from me I felt a need to move closer to be with her. As my body led forward, a powerful forceful hand, centered on my chest, resisted my movement any closer – how could this be? Irene was there and I needed to be next to her. Her smile became even more brilliant while the encircling brightness was beyond belief! With this energy, again, I felt like Irene needed me close to her. Or, was it that I needed to be closer to her? Either way, I attempted to reach and hold my lady, but the strength of the hand, firmly on my chest did not allow me to move closer. What was this about? I don't like it and I am becoming angry. Irene continued to smile as her father's face appeared next to his daughter. Frank Godzik passed in February 1997. Irene, since that day often mentioned how pleased her "daddy" would be as well as proud and happy if he was here with us to spend time with his grandchildren – our children and the three children of Irene's sister, Stasia and her wonderful husband Ed - Kathryn, Sara and Lisa. Every time she spoke these words, it was so painfully clear how much this well-respected, quality man was missed. It was at that moment reality hit me. Irene had passed over. She was with her dad at the right hand of God in the place we know as heaven! But, again, I am supposed to be there as well! With a final push, I attempted to join Irene, Frank and our other deceased loved ones. The strength and resistance on my chest was much more than I could overcome. Irene left this world and the message was clear - she passed to eternity and my world would never be the same. The beauty of the situation was that Irene is totally at peace and happy! To witness my love's joy puts me at an incredible level of peace. Irene will be taken care of and she won't ever feel pain or hurt. Irene is in the presence of an incredibly, resounding place of comfort. It was also clear that I was no way near ready to be with her. I knew my spiritual self was weak, broken and needed enormous repair. It was at that time that I realized how truly loving God is. He loves me so much He gives me another chance at living a life more pleasing to Him.

A moment of more intense warmth and comfort came over me as Irene started to move her lips. My wife's words were clear as she said, "we done good". Such words were ironic as Irene, a teacher, was so articulate with her speech, but, we used this statement each time we talked about our three children, Jennifer, Christopher and Janelle. Irene's lovely face started to fade into the bright, soft sky.

I turned, looked at Irene's lovely face in my hands, gave her a final kiss and told her I would take care of our precious children and would see her again, later, with our God's blessings!

As you continue to read the messages contained in this book, the significance of "LIGHT" in my life cannot be stated enough and with its due respect.

In reflection of your life and as you move on are you conscious of the presence of light, or absence thereof, and what do you see as its significance?

Why bad things happen .....

If God is good why does He allow bad things to happen? This question seems to be a natural reaction when hurt occurs. It certainly was one of my very first. Throughout the world and every moment of the day, bad things happen. Excited, expecting parents find out their child is born and lives for a short time, then passes; a mother and her two children are taking a walk in their neighborhood when hit by a drunk driver and killed; a good athlete is playing in a basketball game, while jumping is fouled and lands in such a way that he is permanently disabled. A successful man heads out to work and once there is told because of a loss in business he no longer has a job; a high school student applies to a certain college and finds out she is not accepted to the school; a knock on the door leaves a military family with one parent as the other is killed in battle. Children are sat down with their parents and told their parents have grown apart and are planning to divorce; at least 2,819 people were killed by the horrific 9 – 11 twin tower attacks, and so on. Where do these experiences begin and end? Do they? Will they? The answer is real – bad things will continue as long as we are in this world.

Evil, grief and agony are a permanent part of our world and are discussed in other parts of this book - the chapter – God, why did you allow this to happen? – is a recap of questions concerning the reality of the sudden passing of my beautiful wife of 27 years and the loving mother of our three wonderful children.

My spiritual growth is based on biblical study and personal experience, which leads me to offer ten statements of reality. I challenge you to your own personal growth and add to this number of messages.

+ God knows what it is to suffer.

Please join me to think about the pain God, our Heavenly Father, felt as His Son cried for help the night before crucified. He knew if He used His power to stop Jesus' suffering, the world would permanently be cursed, without resurrection. Jesus suffered in a human manner. He was persecuted, cursed, mocked, slapped, spit on, stabbed, agonized over anticipated suffering by sweating blood, cried, hurt and was crucified.

+ God is not accountable to me.

The wonders in the world around us are proof enough of God's power. God is in charge and owes me nothing.

+ Choice means much.

God is in a competition with satan over me. One of God's most precious gifts to me is the opportunity of choice. Every choice either honors God or gives in to satan.

+ Look and find the answer.

The Bible is a most valuable resource to understand why bad things happen. There are numerous stories about Christians who faced extreme challenges, and God blessed each with an all new person, as each committed to the Lord. Two specific individuals that showed strength in the eyes of sinful enticement are Job and Paul, they received an abundance of God's love by honoring Him.

+ Above suffering – think not.

Adversity, pain and suffering are part of life. Suffering is an opportunity for growth by turning the challenge over to God. Pain is for gain. I continue to ask Jesus to help me keep perspective of my suffering versus the suffering He endured for me. Also, expecting to avoid suffering would elevate me above God, for He suffered as well.

+ This life versus eternity.

Through a life-changing experience, one of the best lessons was the importance of keeping this life in perspective. Daily blessings surround us – all I need to do is to take the time to enjoy each! This life is a journey leading us to the gates of eternity – God's highest regard for every one of us. Losing my precious wife of 27 years was excruciatingly painful, but with God's blessing of allowing me to witness

Irene's crossover, the hurt was eased. I discuss the gift of strength in this blessing as we move forward

+ Take problems to the Lord.

Life's challenges are an opportunity to honor God by turning them over for Him to handle. No trouble can withstand the power of God. True faith is to trust God when everything seems to be going in the wrong direction. The Bible consistently reinforces that without faith it is impossible to please God. How often do we pray about an issue, then, continue to worry? Why pray if we don't believe God will handle the situation or provide us the wisdom to resolve?

+ It's what we do.

Honoring God, by praying to Him and listening to His direction, is comforting and peaceful. Service to the Lord is leaving a place a bit better, each moment, each day, than we found the situation. Actions that please God are simple and needn't be earth-shattering. Honoring actions are three-fold: doing what He wants us to do, being Christly while doing His will, and enjoying the opportunity to help others grow in their relationship with God as seen in you.

+ From the inside.

When one reflects contentment and happiness, the innerself is in full alignment. The brain and heart are one and the same, revealing a peaceful soul. Thoughts and actions that are honoring to the Lord assure such a peace. Daily time speaking to the Lord for His guidance and understanding creates an atmosphere of this peace, even during the most challenging time.

+ He is in charge.

As I reflect on my life, it is obvious God's will be done. He wants only the best for me as He masterfully designed a plan for my life before I was even born. I reflected on my life and the number of times God's hand had been on me – leading me in one direction while I could have traveled in another. When placing my petitions before our Lord when wrestling with a decision or facing a challenge, during a time of prayer, I have come to enjoy a measure of comfort and peace. As I learned to turn myself over to Him, leaving my life in His hands, the path He has laid out for me becomes clearer and clearer.

A start to find answers .....

To live is to expect, face and battle through challenges. Even as one considers a situation as bleak, hopeless and defeating, the same individual, when truly looking at the whole picture, realizes many good experiences have also contributed to the person's total life. Most often, though, we seem to focus on the negative.

A most valuable resource to contribute to our understanding of oneself and the surrounding world is contained in the most popular book ever written, The Bible. My statement, "This book is the most desired document", is evidenced by the millions upon millions of texts that have been printed, including the versions and written interpretations. Although the actual total number of Bible preparations may be estimated, it is clear, few people dispute no book will ever be written to challenge the document's popularity.

For me, The Bible became the primary source of information enabling my completion of this text. My primary realization, in pursuit of answers to so many questions, The Bible clearly defined the importance of growth in my relationship with a Supreme Being – God.

Once I fully grasped where my life was at the time, I realized a life without a living relationship with God would certainly be undefined and without purpose. In His loving way, God created our world filled with beauty and opportunity; including my life being blessed, for over 29 years, with Irene as well the miraculous gifts as we enjoyed three wonderful children. As I wake every day the evidence of God's love endlessly surrounds us with uniqueness and beauty. Most often, I had never before taken the time to see, appreciate and enjoy each of these special designs.

God's strength is immeasurable. My understanding of why things happen, when, and in the way they do occur, also needed much work.

Question ….. God why did you allow this to happen?

I felt as though I first had to understand Who this being called God is. If He is God, why didn't He just use His power to control this accident from happening? Why doesn't He bring life back into Irene and fix the hurts that our kids with their significant others, Irene's loving sister, Stasia with her family, my family, our mutual friends and I, see and feel. With these questions, I must admit, I feel a certain amount of guilt as I question my role in Irene's passing. As a Catholic, I was taught to accept situations as completely God's work, no matter their relevance to me, and just pray for peace in the outcome. I read of Jesus' repeated acts of miracles during His earthly travels as He resolved situations and cured in the face of the impossible. Considering these works, why wouldn't He do the same, for me, I repeatedly asked?

After reading, listening and watching as the world moves around me, I am constantly reminded everything doesn't just happen. Someone seems to be driving this ship one calls life. This world started somewhere, somehow and its details were too complete for any mere mortal to plan and construct in such detail. For me there had to be an ultimate architect, designer and coordinator for all existence. The answer was clearly the Supreme Being – God.

Other questions then became apparent. Does God exist in me, and if He does, how do I know? How does God look at me in spite of my previous actions, many contrary to His expectations? Did these circumstances happen as a result of my faults, my previous sins? Why did a truly loving God decide on these circumstances in this manner and at this time?

As these questions popped up, it became apparent something was working around and inside of me. I became more driven than ever before to find answers to all these questions. I became a student looking to investigate the deeper meaning about my life. The more I studied, the more I felt an indescribable presence; each answer was purposeful, committed and intense. The words were also amazingly prevalent and pertinent.

Certainly God exists in me. Through the Holy Spirit, His presence is inside of me, I continued to grow with the melding of my mind and heart to create a fulfilled soul. In looking back over the years, I am amazed at the number of times it felt like a force took control of me when I was most in need. Without hesitation I can say I was never alone – even during those times when I felt as though I was on the outside attempting to look or fit in. The times my actions were so far from honoring God there was still a sense of peace that I could make right. By no means does this statement mean, act now and later work it out. In reflection, as I was damaged, by my self-centeredness, selfish act, my life was not ended. Perhaps my conscience and soul were in alignment, together, telling me to learn, keep my eyes on the finish line and stay the course, for there was a reason to look for the answer. At this point, a teaching statement I often used when giving a golf lesson or sharing the challenge of learning with an employee kicked in – learning is the easy part, it is **the un-learning that is so difficult**. As we move forward, this statement's meaning will become that much clearer in this book.

Did my previous faults create the circumstance which was my life at this point? I enjoy comfort in my experience of seeing Irene cross over into eternity and its surroundings. Knowing that God has a plan for me brings my greatest peace. From a human standpoint, my question of whether there would have been a different result if I was driving the vehicle does faintly remain. Also, could I have done a better job of checking out the vehicle's tires before we started out on the trip? And, should I have noticed an abnormality that could have prevented the tire from blowing? Why didn't I research the installation and add a stability bar which may have prevented the vehicle from rolling over? As the auto started to swerve, should I have held on to the steering wheel to keep the vehicle from jolting and rolling? These "what ifs" could continue if I remain centered on my self-perceived control. As my spiritual maturity continues, the Lord knows these questions will answer themselves.

Is God getting back at me? God is fully loving, caring and committed. Through continued growth in His word I know questioning Him in a disrespectful manner is sinful. He knows the deepest meaning of my question as being honoring. He does expect my further, endless maturity in learning and living His word. A minimum feeling of guilt when questioning God, I feel comes from my upbringing to never question Him. Research taught me God desires my questions so I can grow in understanding of Him.

My perception that prayer will always be answered is correct. However, the deepest learning on this topic is the answer may not be what I think it should be and the answer may show itself later than I wanted. This truth is a bit painful, but later this improved understanding continues to prove to be much more fruitful than I could have ever imagined.

During creation God sculptured the making of man and woman, as His special living beings; by distinguishing our worldly presence through a characteristic and special gift He called choice or free will.

The instant Adam and Eve defied God's order "do not partake of the fruit from this tree", the world of total and everlasting **perfection, purity, pleasure, tranquility, health** and **light** ceased to *completely, endlessly* exist.

By the disobedient act of our fellow man and woman, God's creation of a euphoric world ceased to exist for all born. The condition of perfection was introduced to **neglect and fault,** purity - **disarray and filth,** pleasure - **hurt and pain,** tranquility - **chaos and turbulence,** health - **suffering and sickness** while light could become **dim and dark**.

Why, then did God allow this tragedy to happen? Again, as a human being, I was born with the precious gift of choice. However, pain, suffering, darkness and evil are realities of this world and each will stay with me until God's declaration of me on my judgment day. The Bible, a precious, loving gift of our only and true God, is the resource to equip me with the tools to live a complete life and make the most of the cards dealt me. The valuable words contained therein enable me to better understand why an event happens in the manner it does. None of us are exempt from the possibility of being affected by life-challenging events. A change can occur in a split second and can happen at any time, any place and without notice. Again, this happens because our world changed from the perfect world God created. I experienced love and comfort. Why wouldn't I experience pain? I enjoyed light. Darkness exists, as well. There is fantasy. Why wouldn't there be reality? Need I go further? More directly, if I were exempt from varying conditions, of life I would be God. It was in the nature of that consideration the sin of man came into being. We all see how damaging its result.

Let's see how quickly such an experience can occur .....

Please take a little walk with me - who am I to think while being caught up in my daily life anything but the normal day to day would occur? ………. Waking this morning, the same for the last 27 years, next to my lovely wife, taking a quick run outside in the fresh Morehead City, North Carolina, morning air, then jumping out of the shower, quickly dressing, then hugging and kissing my two beautiful daughters, loading the car with our luggage while being blessed with the resources of being able to take a trip, stopping by a restaurant for a quick breakfast, driving a quality automobile on a well maintained highway in a steady flow of traffic, then, suddenly the back, left tire blew and worlds were, literally and completely turned upside down as our vehicle rolled eight times……….. In real life this experience lasted approximately three hours. How long did it take to read this recollection? Whichever position one puts oneself in, the time is minimal in comparison to our family time together. As a reader please take a few seconds and think about that special person, whoever he or she might be and let them know with the best resource at hand, you appreciate him, her or them. For I ask you to consider how truly precious is every moment of one's life? Surely, a situation like this won't happen to you. My mind said the same thing!

With the strongest of reflection, perhaps most enlightening was that this situation is not about a "poor me" syndrome. This painstaking experience opened my eyes to the man reflected in my mirror. Looking into those eyes to the inner self the emptiness was apparent. My world clearly revolved around me as the center. Many of my "accomplishments" were superficial, less than fully rewarding. There appeared to be little I didn't know.

Existing here in this hospital bed my mind continues to float all over the place. **Did this happen because God was getting back at me for my defiance of Him, for sins I committed?** God is all-loving and blessed me with so much. God is not evil and does not deserve to be treated at my human level. Although by His all-encompassing power He is aware of resentment only because He has seen it in man, God does not permit such a state as part of His. It is in my weakness to harbor guilt, a fertile ground for satan to work. As my honor for Jesus Christ's death on the cross for man's sins to be forgiven, upon asking for forgiveness and turning myself completely over to God, will I be released from a state of anything other than that which God created?

The answer of how God looks at me as a reflection of my past actions brings me to the biblical story of a lost sheep. A shepherd would leave his flock of ninety-nine to look for one that has strayed, for the single sheep is at great danger and more vulnerable than those within the flock. I have learned God's love and joy is beyond abundant to one that drifted and then, fully returned to His house. As human beings, our Lord knows we may drift and fall off track. Most pleasing to our Lord is the person who returns to the track, learns from the stumble and shares the message of personal transformation through a noticeable personal change. Again, my concern of how God looks at me is my thought and attempts to reduce Him to my human level of thinking. My real purpose is to honor the Lord, commit to learning and acting in most honoring manner to Him. It is not about my analysis of what God is thinking. It is the doing to learn His true purpose for me and fulfilling this special plan.

This revelation led me to the point a light finally started to go on within me. Why did it take such a life-changing event for me to begin to open the door to the true meaning and purpose of life? This answer is painstakingly clear – I was so wrapped up in my own life that I couldn't see the forest through the trees. Admittedly, this reality did not come without hours and hours of arguing with myself, with God and others that were in front of me when the mood struck. Personal growth and improvement, whether emotional, physical or spiritual, can be a painstaking endeavor, especially when one is so hard-headed and resistant to the truth that more often than not is as clear as clear can be. Again, to me, answers to the most challenging in nature, most difficult to understand and seemingly unanswerable questions are contained in the book of truth.

For only through an unconditional, unending, unfailing love would any being persist on knocking at the same door until a response occurs. God loves me so deeply that He continued to use lesson upon lesson until I got the message of His calling to me.

The pain of losing Irene as well as seeing our beautiful children suffer with deep grief from her passing is hurtful beyond belief. However, we were all so blessed to have had this special lady touch our lives in a limitless number of ways – along with the birth of Jen, Chris and Janelle, are examples of His love for me.

You, too, are a child of God – filled with His same love and blessings. Please join me in realizing and sharing with others just how special each one of us is to our Almighty Father!

Could this be why God provided the powerful words for the document that survived challenge after challenge from the most acclaimed scholars, seemingly from every corner of the world, and through the complete existence of time?

Part of our family: The Ogorzaleks, Grandma Godzik Sharpe,
Jen, Janelle, Heather, Chris, Irene & I.

Life Changes....Forever!

A fun time
with Irene!

Colomb family photo

Above, Reggie Colomb
walks out of the rehab
center on an emotional
day in Wilmington. At
left, the Colomb family
(from left: Reggie,
Janelle, Irene, Chris and
Jennifer) pose during a
family trip to Scotland.

With Chris on his wedding day!

With Jen and Janelle, in my wheelchair.

Me with my good friend, Dr. John Liguori.

A smile with Eula and Barbara – true blessings!

Light from darkness ….. *seven precious words* …..

The beauty and comfort of being witness as a cherished loved one crosses over from this life to eternity provides a level of peace in spite of the reality of the devastating loss. This opportunity represented a direction to share the message DEATH IS A NEW LIVING, A MOST PRECIOUS GIFT FROM OUR ALMIGHTY CREATOR. Yes, the pain associated with experiencing death of the most precious beings in our lives, such as spouse or child, creates excruciating hurts of seemingly immeasurable proportion. However, knowing she or he will never again feel pain, will only enjoy a height of pleasure we are unable to comprehend and she or he will forever live in the perfect home setting is comforting assurance at the most tremendous level!

Also, know that we will be afforded the opportunity to be with this departed love for eternity when we pass ourselves! These words are not just said. Our loving Father, God, promised eternity for those who live His word. As our most trusted relative and loved one - GOD KEEPS PROMISES, FULLY! The Bible outlines "the light, the way and the path to be with Him".

Be assured, your loss will be forever a part of you. There will be days when the hurt and pain associated with missing that special someone will engulf your thoughts and total self. Heck,that is love!   I encourage you to find a place of solitude, pray to Jesus and share your thoughts about your loved one with Him or speak to your love as God knows where you are, is with you and through

His love will enable a connect deeper than you can ever imagine! Again, please be reminded, God felt pain too and He cried from the hurt of death. God knows and cares! He also instilled a peace within me I never thought possible. Simply, all I need to do is ask Him for help and He does. He thrives on being asked and trusted as my answer!

Upon reflection of a day in the hospital, there is a particular moment which will help me reinforce the message of eternity. During the most challenging times in our lives, a truth about our fellow man often becomes apparent. At this time, the simplest word can have a lasting effect. Each day Jen, Chris and Janelle would read me cards and messages of love from family and friends. One particular card was signed by members of my then employer, The Country Club of the Crystal Coast. Janelle, read the messages highlighted by the words, *"He is the light of the world"*, signed Jackie and Clive. Jackie Luckenbill, a good friend, would, from time to time, share conversation with me discussing God's messages in our lives. The word "light", once again hit a nerve. Later that same day Jen graciously repeated the words as the feelings of peace and warmth filled the same heart that was feeling the effects of losing my wife - empty and lifeless. Those special words again changed the direction and course of a shattered heart.

As time continued to pass, it became apparent of my need and desire to explore the true meaning of why the **_seven words_** - *He is the light of the world* - had and continue to have such a dramatic impact on my inner self.

Reconnecting to my inner-self…..

The realism that my life will never be the same is becoming clearer. A wonderful person was brought into my life and helped me have a deeper understanding of personal love – patience, kindness, support, honor, acceptance, understanding and a continuous number of words beyond my current vocabulary, to describe the lady I was no longer going to close my eyes with and wake beside.

I feel as though I am alone for the very first time in over thirty years. With this message I am challenged to look at my inner-self, and the view of my shallowness is unquestionable. Irene and I had spoken about what each of us wanted for the other when the time came for our lives to separate by death, but, that was supposed to be after our 110th birthdays and at least after our 75th anniversary. Clearly, though, another plan was established and in my current state I question what the future has in store. Right now I am uncertain and dreadfully afraid of being alone. Also, I am tremendously anxious about becoming a burden to Jen, Chris and Janelle, our three children and their families. For this reason alone I feel as though I need to completely rebuild my inner-self in every aspect of my being.

It is truly amazing as I begin to lay out a sort of game plan within my head of how every past experience in my life has a clearer definition and how it relates to my current circumstance. I use the word amazing because of the simplicity of those past moments, yet realizing the complexity and clarity to today.

As I began reading the many books received as gifts, the words led to the same starting place for my re-construction. On Sundays I listen to various sermons by Joel and Victoria Osteen, Dr. Charles Stanley and Joyce Myers, as their messages meld perfectly to so many written words. My ability to become more complete had to start at the most fundamental aspect of me. To move on it is important to realize and grasp my life's new purpose.

As days continued to go by a hidden force drew me to visit other patients within the same wing of this hospital – New Hanover Medical Center. The patients suffered from spinal, brain and other serious injuries. Each morning, after sneaking a little extra gym time, I visited patient rooms to say prayers for patients in other rooms. My feeling was that if I could contribute to converting negative situations by demonstrating constant hope with a positive attitude, while also working to show consistent physical improvements myself, all of our world would be improved and somewhat better. Also, I learned to believe that praying for others with others, as repeatedly declared by various spiritual messengers and throughout the Bible is tremendously pleasing to God, drawing me even closer to Him. The power of prayers is discussed throughout this book. My purpose, though, is not about me, but rather to brighten my fellow patients' day. Being a CMA club manager and PGA golf professional for nearly thirty years, provided me plenty of experience in appreciating the importance and results of fresh, positive air, which Irene and I committed to maintaining in our own home so our children would feel good about themselves. Simply, we felt positive air meant positive results and positive results meant inner power. Jen, Chris and Janelle clearly demonstrated this strength during the challenging time as their mom left this world and passed to eternity in a tragedy.

And, assisting others during their challenging times became another motivating purpose for me to move on each day. The tools to be able to accomplish great things and God's true purpose are built on the foundation of a clear, peaceful mind and cleansed heart - a complete soul.

My previous life taught me many lessons - one of the most valuable being - there are no more "takeovers or mulligans." Also, it is clear someone was watching over me to endure maturing situations and allow me a NEW CHANCE to a more complete, fulfilling life. My need is to totally commit to the real prize life has to offer. For now, I spend days and nights taking personal inventories and evaluations on the topic called – Rege.

Through journaling, I reflect on my younger life – my kid days and my pre-Irene days. With these assessments I was able to see the full value of a true life partner – one who knew every intimate detail about me – my thoughts and actions, day in and day out. What took me so long to realize was this being was my hidden protection from myself, as well as a defining presence to my future self. Yet, immobility with a lost path inhibited my complete person to be formed. Present, were gaping holes, stubbed toes and blistered hands. It is apparent now, just how self-centered and self-indulging I was then. Those experiences, however, will provide me the platform from which to share with others that may be traveling along a similar detour to reclaim the original, truly intended path, for each our lives.

My need for a spiritual awakening is where it is at and the answer to a renewed life and fulfillment of purpose. Throughout the Bible are an endless number of personal accounts with people of all walks of life reflecting on this same new found energy, based on the in-depth meaning of truly living.

An appreciation for the simplest aspects of life such as the sparkle and fresh taste of a sip of water, the brilliance of seeing the crispness in a rain drop and the invigorating energy in a deep breath of a morning's fresh air mustn't be lost and each represents daily gifts I now appreciate more than ever!

The How to .....

Before fully learning the *why to* it was clear the *how to* explore my spiritual inner-self and develop it was just as important for me. I needed to understand a greater appreciation for this life and how come things happen why and when they do.

Again, listening to different people that seemed to be at peace with themselves, praying and the precious words of the Bible – two words kept sticking in my brain, to the point of being consistently asked how I could smile each time I spoke of our tragedy and seem positive. Without thought those two words slid from my mouth – Holy Spirit. The words flowed out with little understanding of what the words really meant. Truly, the words came out of nowhere quicker than any words I had ever used.

To understand the Holy Spirit it was important for me to learn how that being fit with God and Jesus Christ. Simply, God is my creator and is all powerful. He is the supreme. Jesus Christ was a form of God that walked the earth as man for me to better understand God's expectations in human actions and terms, then died on the cross, rising from this death so I may be able to live without the burden of previous, permanent sin. Prior to Jesus' death the words of God were spoken as a promise of a precious gift as **guidance** to live my life in an honoring manner - hence, the Holy Spirit.

The Holy Spirit is my *how to* know and feel God's presence in my life. Prior to making every decision I first have the opportunity to think about my response while my heart provides me a feeling prior to actually making the decision. The combination of thought and feeling may lead to my response. What I have now learned is that prior to deciding, if I take a bit of additional time, a more important element of me will lead to the decision that is best for me. This aspect of my decision is the Holy Spirit working. His presence is God's affirmation the decision is best to fulfill the ultimate plan for my life. At times, the decision may lead to a result that I may not have expected and could appear to be other than what I think is the best; but it is the decision that is best for the long term fulfillment of God's ultimate plan for me. This approach challenges the word FAITH to its fullest extent. However, I am assured that since my decision is based on the Holy Spirit (God's presence within me) God is pleased that I am honoring Him. As the Bible says throughout – actions most pleasing to God will bring great rewards. My life, today, is a testimony to just that. When I was in my darkest moments there appeared to be nowhere else for me to turn and it was at that time **God's greatest work occurred in me!**

Some may view the Holy Spirit as conscience, but, his, presence is deeper. The Holy Spirit is beyond my true ability to reason – the **Holy Spirit is reminding, guiding, leading, directing** and **empowering** me. In total, the **Holy Spirit is comforting**.

Please be assured, if I can improve on my ability to soul search and connect, based on where I have been, you can certainly become more at peace with yourself than you could ever have imagined by applying this same practice before making crucial life decisions. Your life and the lives of people around you will be more fulfilled and so many more good things will happen. God's promises and examples of His keeping these are throughout the Bible with repetition in the lives of so many today!

The Why to …..

There were so many reasons why it was important for me to seek spiritual growth and understanding. First, as you will read, so many times in my life there was a force, energy and an element inside of me that I truly did not ever think about until a most significant tragedy affected my perspective on life. I took for granted an internal something that watched over. The opportunity to wake up, jump out of bed, take a morning run or walk, kiss my wife and kids, head out to work, and all the other wonderful things that form a day, were all taken for granted and without my true appreciation for each.

With so much time to think, one of the "why to" was for me to understand that something that I am convinced is inside of every one of us. Please take a moment – do you realize just how truly fortunate you are to be where you are and have all you have, right now? Again, I did not at a critical time in my life. Therefore, please be invited to appreciate the special everythings that are part of you! This perspective alone may answer *the why* for you. For me, I needed to delve further.

Through prayer, listening to message carriers, reading the Bible and testing the information, the picture became clearer and clearer. As you read on you will see the importance of growth. I challenge you to at least give yourself the chance to go beyond your granted gifts to see importance of understanding *the why* for yourself.

Rebuilding a relationship …..

My study of the Bible continues to teach me the greatness of God. The central message of this great book is God loves me and wants to forgive me. The Bible teaches me valuable lessons …..

….. God is all forgiving and He has made the way back to Him clear

Initially, it was apparent for me to understand the depth and intensity of God's love for me. Again, evidence of this love is all around me. The pain from the loss of Irene and seeing the hurt on the faces of our children is clear. Later my writing will address this topic at length. The point that God loves me is apparent as He brought me to see Irene as she passed from this life. Seeing her beautiful smile as her brilliance reflected peace and joy gave me the chance to be at peace, as well. Also, through God's love He enabled me to see where Irene is and realize His desire for me to enter that same place and its opportunity.

God's love is unconditional. The words of the Bible clearly state regardless of where my being is at any time He wants me for His own. It brought me peace to understand that God, Himself, is selfish. He wants me for Himself and sharing my being with satan, through sin, is a hateful feeling God has. I realized God demonstrates humanity. He has feelings. God feels hurt and pain. Each time my actions were of a sinful nature, God was hurt.

God came to earth through the birth of His son, Jesus. Jesus lived a human life. Through God's order and in Jesus' love, this Man accepted the responsibility, knowingly, to endure incredible human emotional and physical pain ending in death, by being nailed to a cross. During His time of enduring man-inflicted pain Jesus was stuck with a spear. As my thoughts centered on this, my vision brought me to the point to think of my actions. During my life, am I helping to remove this weapon or is this spear being twisted, inflicting even more pain, by the selfish acts of my continued sinning? For the endless number of blessings that I've enjoyed during my life, how can I continue to add to His pain? He died the most precious of all deaths, and did so filled with love for me. Then, three days later Jesus rose from this death in resurrection and therefore, redemption for sin, including mine.

Only through realizing the MOST AMAZING DISPLAY OF UNCONDITIONAL LOVE would I begin to understand how and why this MIRACLE could happen and realize how truly loved I am.

Then to be enlightened to the path back to God's endless grace, precious biblical words outlined the how to. The realism is that God knows everything, including all about me – where I've been, all my actions and still loves me! He has a **master plan** for my life which I will outline later in this writing. Now for my opportunity to better understand this life.

First, it was up to me to seek Christ to confess my sins. Seeking Christ is speaking from the heart, in prayer, with or without the presence of another person, and confessing sin. This prayer can be as simple as – Christ Jesus, I ask you to hear my prayer as I tell you my actions against you. Trust in Jesus, who in His love and kindness without reservation takes away our sins. His death on the cross was restitution for our sins so that the guilt held inside is released. Speaking through Jesus is stated in the Bible to speak to God. God is anxious and ready to forgive sin. He may be more ready to forgive my sin that I may be prepared to ask Him for forgiveness.

Let me share another perspective of God's forgiveness. I looked at forgiveness naturally, through my human eyes. I now have a much deeper understanding of God's willingness to forgive. For me, it became my "capability" to forgive, while our Loving Father forgives without limit or condition according to His forgiving nature. He is our loving, non- contrite Creator.

God's willingness to forgive cannot be imagined – through faith we learn to accept and realize His strength in any situation cannot be measured. I know His love for me, and desire to have me completely under His fold is greater than I am capable of seeing myself being. Through my own shame my perspective of self-worth for God' love is shaded and gray. Daily prayer and reading His word brings light to the situation as a new opportunity to better understand my need to forgive in order to be truly forgiven.

Following my prayer through Jesus, thanking God for His forgiveness is the next step. Instead of continually asking for forgiveness, I need to continually thank God for the forgiveness which has already been received because He promises to forgive. I had to realize through God's strength He only needs to be asked for forgiveness one time. He is more centered on my living as a reflection of His love than in remembering my acts against Him.

It is clear God keeps no record of wrongs. As humans we often get caught up on this reaction. My prayer also includes asking Jesus to help me release myself from the guilt of sins. Through this prayer, the Holy Spirit shows me by holding on to regretful actions, I am placing myself above God, and in doing so, the release would not occur with future long days becoming longer. Again, God is a gracious and all-forgiving God. His will is done!

Beginning to rebuild my life, my thoughts and actions centered on our Almighty Father, is the foundation. Through daily prayer and continued study of His word, my life's purpose is clarified while the Holy Spirit fills me with the feeling of assurance that I am on the right path! This feeling may be the connection between my conscience thinking and subconscious soul which defines my honor to God as my character.

Place called Heaven …..

By seeing the smile on her face as she passed, I know Irene is in a better place. What have I learned about this place called heaven?

Through my reading the Bible it became my understanding "heaven" may be the place where God began His creation. His is the perfect place – comfortable and pain free; clean without stain; happy, sadness free; bright exempt from darkness, and so on….. Its location - physically, heaven can be anywhere as it is another reflection of our God's endless power. I point to the sky when speaking of heaven as a human signal to be at God's feet and look up to all that He is and represents.

Heaven is eternal, everlasting life. It is the whereabouts when my physical life comes to an end. Today's life, then, is the first part of my journey – the preliminary golf tournament leading to the permanent championship place where all participants are trophy holders.

Heaven is the result of honoring God and fulfilling His plan, of pleasing our Father. It is the place of hope, direction and value as my belief strengthens. The hope is that when called to leave this physical world through death, my journey will be to rejoin Irene and all other loved ones that have also passed and honored God during their lives on earth. This hope is a motivating strength to continue living. Heaven represents the direction for living a life fulfilling His plan for me. The value that there is a greater meaning to our worldly existence also defines the heavenly path.

God, the only being that truly keeps His full word and promises, declared eternity as our purpose. Through faith I trust God's plan for me as my path to heaven and assurance to a life here-after filled with everything that is **great beyond human understanding!**

Heaven can be viewed as a guidepost, a lighthouse, a directional aid to an airplane while in flight. By surrendering my life to Jesus and renewing my heart to His way, my purpose is of priceless proportion. All my fluttering about, thinking only of my desires and needs, a more self-centered state of my life I demonstrated prior to being led to a new life is no longer me. The brightness I saw around Irene as she passed is my focus – the guidepost of my living – **the Light of Direction** to eternity.

As you think of heaven, regardless of the circumstance leading you to think about "the place", please know its entrance is a place of immeasurable beauty, comfort and warmth. I experienced during my blessing of seeing Irene cross over. **With its entrance being so perfect, how miraculous is the final destination?!**

Challenges ….

Reflecting on my time in a hospital bed, unable to feel much of anything other than hurts in my heart; my mind raced through the realisms of this current place in my life as the world continues to move around me. I attempt to process this situation while my mind, with fear, struggles to understand my new world.

This new world will assuredly be filled with an increasing number of challenges, both emotional and physical. At this point I believed that if I can unlock the key to confronting the emotional issues, the physical challenges may be a bit easier to face and hurdle over, under, around or through.

Holding the family together, with the devastating loss of our family glue, Irene's mothering, endless love demonstrated by her limitless patience and understanding appears to be the biggest challenge. It is apparent Jen, Chris and Janelle have a strong bond. Heather, Chris' fiancé, is also an integral part of our family. It is nice to think the values and family environment Irene and I worked to create helped to establish a foundation for their love to continue. To me, the best thing I feel I can do is to work hard to avoid adding to their burden and stress.

The other challenges are real:

- The sudden loss of the wonderful mother of our children and seeing them hurt speaks for itself.

- The departing of the lady I thought was to be my life partner and best friend – my heart's void and emptiness is painful beyond belief.
- My physical changes – a permanently injured, curved spine with shattered, twisted ribs and hip and knee damage have left a vain guy with constant pain as well as a battle to accept my changed appearance. Being tossed through a vehicle window also weakened my body and will require much work so that my stamina can be increased.
- Mobility is non-existent – is it true a permanent life in wheelchair is ahead for this guy?
- Overcoming my need for heavy medication is also tremendously important to me. During my life, rarely did I ever take medication other than an occasional flu shot. My body never did well in accepting medications, but, at this point, my physical damage dictates the need for their use. Down the road my goal is to minimize, if not eliminate, medication use.
- Within a short time I realized my first major battle – accepting the need, at that point, for my children to change and clean me. The pain of exchanging places with my son as he placed a diaper on his dad depicts a depth of my life that no man should experience. Moving forward I converted this pain to fuel inner drive that only a loving, true God provides. Feeling the love of my children also contributes as a heightened, motivating element.

- As days passed new challenges started to present themselves – would I be able to return to work? Financially, how will I be able to afford paying bills? Will I be able to provide Janelle further education as we had for Jen and Chris? Where and how would I live daily? On and on the questions continued to hit me …..

Irene's impact on my life will be constantly reflected in this communication and cannot possibly be stated fully. Irene was one of those rare people who never said an ill word of anyone. She always saw the good in people and reflected a kind, gentle self. For now, the real picture is that Irene is physically no longer here and that is painful.

The hurt I see on the faces of our children is just simply not supposed to be there. Just a short time ago we were all sitting in the living room, together, enjoying pizza and laughing at some ridiculous "reggie- ism". Irene, shrugging her shoulders, smiling and winking at Jen, Chris, Janelle and Heather and would say, "that's your dad and we love him for him". Now, though, their young, but, battered faces reflect a pain and helplessness tremendously difficult to see. After all, as Jen often said, "we know when we needed a certain word and protection, dad, you were there". Now, I feel this statement is way too far from the truth. I ask why can't I just stand up, hold each of my children and make things back to the way they had been?

As the medical prognosis was grim, the words were I would not walk again, body movements would be limited, at best, and a life in a wheelchair was inevitable. This is a far distance from an active, physical self, even though a bit out of shape, my recent mornings began with a run or speedy walk around our neighborhood, Brandywine Bay. Some mornings, preparing a family breakfast and the girls' lunch, taking Janelle to school, followed by a call to Irene telling her the daily message that the package had been delivered. She would respond with a teasing comment of her own, as I then headed to my challenges of managing a country club – The Country Club of the Crystal Coast. After tackling the tasks at hand, working with our course superintendent Andy Ipock, Lorraine DiJoseph,our administrative manager, Troy Forguites in the pro shop and Jennifer the membership program coordinator, it was time to enjoy striking a few balls prior to or following golf lessons, either to a group of our ladies, or a daily swing fix with a club member and good friend Everette Edwards. Then even playing a round of golf with my buddies Phil Panzarella, Glen Mills and Steve Robinson or other club members, it was time to call it the end of a work day. On the way home, Irene and I chatted about her day and our plans for dinner, along with the evening ahead! All and all, I am in a struggle to understand how a relatively active guy can be so easily relegated to immobility and nearly total insufficiency.

As I continue to try to figure out what is truly going on, many other circumstances are constantly swirling in my head. I search to understand if it is true I will not physically feel. Have you ever desired to feel a pain in any part of your body? What I would give to wake up with a leg cramp or muscle spasm. Also, it is so hard for me to believe when nature calls for me to go to the bathroom, it will just happen and I will be in the position of waiting for a diaper change just as I had done for my younger brothers, sister and children when each was an infant. Will I again fulfill the roll of being a dad? Or, will I be a permanent burden to our kids? Once out of this bed, what will I look like? The thought that is intently vibrating in my head and heart is lack of my presence during the time when our children, family and friends bid farewell to Irene from this world to eternity during her Catholic Mass and burial, back in Rutland, Vermont, our hometown. It is tremendously painful to know she has passed, but, shouldn't I have had the chance to say good bye alongside our children?

And, from time to time my mind searches to understand where me, as a broken person, emotionally and physically, is headed. Obviously, there is a new life ahead of me, but, what is it? Will it be purpose or burden?

Time alone …..

The thought of being alone never entered my mind as this reality has hit me in my deepest and whole heart. Reading and listening became my greatest outlet, aside from seeing and holding my children, and became my primary life functions during early rehabilitation.

It was during this time my personal need became glaring. Through constant thoughts of guilt and things I should have done differently while Irene was still with me, my spiritual weakness showed itself clearer to me than anything else could have. Through all my hurts, a sense of comfort filled me from head to toe every time the word of God was in my day. I felt the same synergy throughout my body that I mentioned when writing about the experience of witnessing Irene's crossover and the view of seeing the birth of Jen, Chris and Janelle.

Getting to the point of this growth was, and continues to be, a process. So many questions seemed without reason or answer. At first during my commitment to find answers it was remarkable how often my query was answered in an unexpected place and time. Today, I know that doesn't just happen and is part of a true master plan! The answers are truly the work of our Almighty Father! All I ever needed to do was ask – watch, listen and keep my lips closed. For those who knew the other Reggie this sounds much easier than it was. Why does one need to learn when he already has all the answers?

One of my initial questions was **how do I know God wants me with all my past faults and sins?**

God wants all of us for His own. His desire is that every person enters eternity upon their passing. This statement is profound, but true, as evidenced by God's initial creation of our world and man. The Bible clearly states God's disappointments when our fellow man (and woman), Adam and Eve, ate the forbidden fruit. God established forgiveness by sending His only son to live with the same man (and woman) who defied His direction. Jesus traveled this earth and experienced human feelings of every nature prior to dying the most horrific death by being nailed to a cross. Three days later our Lord Jesus Christ fulfilled His Father's order when he rose from the dead as Redemption of this sin of man and laid the path for each of us to follow so we can enjoy an eternal life, even after our physical death.

Words of the Bible state we are forgiven so long as we are willing to forgive. Often, we miss the opportunity to fully appreciate God's forgiveness because we have a difficult time forgiving ourselves. We hold on to our past shortcomings and sins. As we ask the Father for His forgiveness, because he has no memory, God immediately releases each of us simply by asking, then thanking Him and acting in a more mature manner in the future.

It is apparent God loved and desired for me to fully turn to Him when He spared my life and **gave me a second chance at this life,** with an opportunity for my soul to enjoy eternity along with Irene and all others that have passed. As Irene passed over, our Loving Father knew I was not ready and honoring to His expectations and therefore my life was spared. God was not done with me and has further plans for me.

A next question seemed to be a natural. **How do I strengthen my relationship with God?**

I need to remember to have as short a memory as Him. Again, He has no memory of previous sins. He sees me with my current and future actions so long as each is not hurtful to my relationship with Him. His gracious memory does not release me from being accountable for my sins. This statement means once my petition for forgiveness is placed before God, He is all-loving and does not remember this past sin. God's might ensures His full awareness of my sincerity when asking for forgiveness.

Ten (10) steps of my action enable strong relationship with our Supreme Father:

1. Through Jesus, speak with an open mind and heart using the words that work for me to convey my message or petition. God understands the meaning of my words.
2. Acknowledge, with full truth, my sin against God and His world.
3. Ask for forgiveness and every time ask for the strength to forgive others, including myself.
4. Thank Jesus for His death on the cross as the ultimate opportunity for me to be forgiven.

5. Through a profound Love of God make every attempt to avoid future sin, understanding we are human and sin is inevitable.

6. Continue to study God's word through the Bible and other resources.

7. Demonstrate His way by my improved actions and words.

8. Share God's word and make that a mission of my life.

9. Lead others to God and accept persecution from the non-believer, and remain steadfast to Him and His word.

10. Thank God for all His blessings. Let me be reminder of the simplest example of God's constant love for me.

This process is a way of life and continues to transform my commitment and constant growth.

From here, where do I begin to understand my new life's purpose?

As each day passed one of God's strongest messages to me was that life is about purpose. Its returns and riches are measured by my inner-peace and certainty of fulfilling the plan God defined for me. Unfortunate as it may appear; too many days were lost until I realized life is not about me but rather making me available to demonstrate God's work. To clarify this viewpoint – life's purpose is fulfilled by where we are right now by demonstrating God's presence in everything we do. It is unbelievably amazing to think that God established a plan for every one of us well before our birth. He knew that I would need more work than many others until His way is clearer to me. Again, with His endless love, God did not give up on me. Rather, He kept tapping me on the head as the picture became clearer and until this lost sheep was found and brought back to the fold by the Shepherd. I have learned how pleased this makes God, and know the riches He has planned for me continue to unfold and present themselves. A full understanding of God's purpose for me is a constant work as well. I continue to learn by realizing:

1. God has a perfectly orchestrated plan for my life.
2. I am a special being and hand-picked by Him to do His work.
3. Peace and comfort exist in turning my life completely over to God so He will work in me.
4. The importance of constant work to solidify my strong relationship with Him.
5. To allow God to work in me by listening more and speaking less. Anyone that knew me knows how difficult this really is!
6. How to appreciate all of God's work around me.
7. It is imperative to praise Him by using prayer and actions to honor His being.
8. Challenging myself to go as far as I can go with every challenge and opportunity He presents to me.
9. And understanding once my actions have taken their full course He will take over from there until the end result is His.
10. There is a new me and I am to thank God for every opportunity to grow in His name!

How do I know when I am connected with God?

A deeper understanding of God's being helps me to feel confidence and comfort of His presence. He exists in three beings – Himself, as Father, Jesus Christ His son, and the Holy Spirit. As Father, God is our supreme ruler, designer and total everything. Jesus Christ was God's form on earth as the Father's son. He experienced the world through man's eyes. Jesus was born as we are born, in a much more meager setting, lived life as a youth and grew to be the only perfect man before He was persecuted for His commitment to the Father and ultimately was crucified to redeem me. To connect to the Father, in the Bible Jesus says we must go through Him to be able to enjoy God's blessings.

The Holy Spirit is God's presence within me. He is my spiritual conscience and as I hear His voice, know God and I are connected. The more I work to understand God, the clearer the Holy Spirit messages become. I believe the Holy Spirit's home is my soul, the deepest unity of my heart and brain, the sum of my conscious thought and internal feeling.

The Bible tells me there are seven primary gifts of the Holy Spirit that help me shape my response to life's circumstances:

1. **Wisdom** – our belief through faith. Faith is my internal self by the contributing factors of my desire, vision, openness, acceptance and appreciation for the world and its contents around me. As these attributes exist my faith is present.

2. **Understanding** – is the willingness and ability to know spiritual truths. To be able to understand I have to continue to work at finding meaning in a deeper sense.

3. **Direction** – the guidance of that little voice that helps me act in a manner that is pleasing to God. My decisions.

4. **Courage** – my inner self that drives me to go forward and is my ever developing strength to try and move on in spite of the external forces that attempt to work against me, even when I am unaware of their existence.

5. **Knowledge** – based largely on experience, at this point, this may be my best means to accelerate the successful life of honoring Him and enjoying its blessings.

6. **Faithfulness** – my commitment to honor God by serving Him. By realizing the enormous number of blessings in my life, my desire to serve the Lord is my daily driving force. My true understanding of the meaning of "to LOVE and to be LOVE(D)" is God's greatest presence and gift.

7. **Respect** – the Holy Spirit is the conscious desire not to offend God and knowing each time I do sin against Him my inner-self is unsettled and disrupted.

Although my time alone is difficult, unsettled and scary, its rewards continue to help me grow and understand more than I would have ever been able to imagine. This dark period has challenged me to look at myself in the deepest way and clearly reinforces God's presence (light) is most astounding during the darkest periods of my life. **During these times it is apparent HE IS THE WAY AND THE LIGHT.** As Jesus continued in the Bible, **"I am the way and the**

Light. He who believes in me shall never die, but, will experience Everlasting Life."

Why ...... a cross?

Cross stems from a latin word – crux, cruciare – meaning to torture. The symbol may be viewed as Jesus suffering and dying for man's sin.

The cross is a symbol employed by almost every culture throughout the world with different meanings. It is viewed with a world center and cosmic axis. With its human form it projects four cardinal points, fourfold systems: the four directions – north, south, east and west; four seasons – spring, summer, fall and winter, four daily guides for doing the right thing – *"please forgive me"*, *"I forgive you"*, *"thank you"* and *"I love you"*, other fours ...... etc.

On a deeper interpretation the cross symbolizes a commonality that points to a significance at the *intersection* of two lines. Spiritually, does God use this point to reflect change **good** from evil, **light** from dark, **new life** from the past, **forgiveness** from sin?

Cross-bearing goes with the Christian life. There is no life without a cross. Jesus never spoke of His death apart from His **victory** over it. As Christians we should never look at the present cross apart from the **promised crown**.

Our minds should be made up to accept the cross as an opportunity to win the crown. A cross rejected is satan's instrument of torture. A cross thankfully accepted is Christ's training for the great triumph of **eternal life**.

Let us remember when we have crossed a brook of challenge, and look back, there is joy even in pain and suffering as we know God will **make everything work together for our good**. He has promised this to us and God is the only man one who constantly, completely keeps His word.

God's chastening's (works) are as much a part of His faithfulness as His blessings. In God's plan, cross-bearing and crown-wearing go together.

Jesus walked this earth as man and accepted the pain of suffering. He suffered the same aspects as man – emotionally and physically. His spiritual suffering was also beyond human comprehension since Jesus did so completely for everyone other than Himself – for each of us!

Together, let's now explore this symbol of Christianity – the cross.

In the Bible, Jesus said, "If anyone wishes to be a follower of mine, he must take up his cross and come with Me".

Crosses come in many sizes. The cross that burdens God's children also comes in a great variety of forms.

Cross of heredity

Through our solidarity and birth through Adam and Eve, we face the common ills of humanity. Millions are born blind, deaf, dumb, and with other mental and physical defects. If at birth we escape major genealogical maladies, we are to be thankful. But we may not boast. Our cross will come in time.

Cross as the direct action of satan

Jesus traced illness to satan's power. Often we make wrong choices as we set aside God's written, precious guidance each time we live in the moment of self-satisfaction. An endless number of people find themselves guilty of the syndrome of "if only I had" or "if only I hadn't".

Biological crosses

Any one of hundreds of virulent germs can enter the body to bring sickness and pain. Cells go astray to create a malignancy. The bloodstream is poisoned. A respiratory system fails. The nerves storm about. Calcium deposits bring on arthritis. These conditions are a way of life. How does a child die of brain cancer? A tremendous athlete hits the ground, dying of a heart attack. A beautiful mother of three leaves this world suddenly. All these situations are proof that a foreign power caused havoc in God's once serene and perfect order.

Sociological crosses

Our society is excellent at creating evil, but cannot control it. People in their natural state are filled with injustice, mischief, cruelty and malice. Envy, murder, rivalry, treachery and nastiness are people's acts that cause hurt to others. Not one of us can escape the hurt and anguish resulting from gossip, bad temper, malice, selfishness and revenge. A bleeding heart hurts as much as a bleeding body.

Self-imposed and psychological crosses

Through ignorance, excesses, or disregard for basic health rules people sponsor their own sorrow. They work themselves to death, worry to the point of sickness, smoke too much, drink too much or take dangerous drugs. The works of the flesh: fornication, impurity, indecency, idolatry, quarrels, envy, fits of rage, selfish ambitions, dissensions and jealousy, are not only bad, they are bad for us.

Crosses of empathy

Assuming ownership of another's burden lays the groundwork for the empathetic cross. Unless we have a heart of stone we face the possibility of carrying another's burden. Let us understand, by loving and caring for another, their cross can become our own. The anguish of parents whose child becomes hooked on drugs or someone saddened to hear the escapades of a friend who is having an extramarital affair are examples of crosses of empathy, which may be the heaviest of all.

Christian-witnessed crosses

Few Christians will avoid the cross of their faith as satan is constantly working to transform the believer into a sinful creation. This is satan's lifeline and purpose. The Bible states, "All that will live godly shall suffer persecution".

Our cross is Lightened by God's Cross

How often do we take moment by moment blessings for granted, yet, question God when a challenge of any velocity confronts us? When Jesus came to earth He very much lived a human life. And, when called to fulfill His purpose suffered beyond a point any man could have endured.

As our heavenly Father, God knows each pain everyone suffers.

It was in the suffering of his Son that God drew closest to man. It is still in suffering that God continues to be near His children.

Our most challenging moments are also our greatest opportunities to grow with our Lord.

In our suffering God's hands are always open, His heart goes out to us and through the Holy Spirit we are caught, should we quiver and start to fall.

There can be no life without a cross. Jesus never spoke of pain, suffering and death without reinforcing His victory and promised peace and joy. As we continue to grow in spiritual strength we are assured every cross is a path to ultimate comfort in God's domain. When we hold on to the elements of pain with bitterness and self-pity we send an invitation to satan leading to continued torture. A cross graciously accepted is a medal of appreciation and loving response from us to God.

A Thought About Pain …..
While in the hospital or during follow up visits with doctors, more often than not, the initial question asked is, "How is your pain"? I appreciate the loving tone by the inquiry of these important

people in my life. Few did not mention their observation was that my pain tolerance level was extremely high.

When I did think about pain my mind would go to two observations mentioned earlier in this text. One, Jesus' preparation and eventual death on the cross for a cause He accepted, but, had not caused its necessity in any way, shape or form. And, secondly, the statement that pain is weakness leaving the body. The more I thought about this statement, the more truthful it became.

Certainly, I am far from a hero and my approach helped me to put my pain in perspective. Please understand my body was hurting, constantly and deeply. But, during my visits with patients before discharge and to this day, the memory of my pain quickly subsides to a tolerable level.

For me, emotional pain may be the "deepest" pain of all. Often, emotional pain is latent with guilt, question, anger, uncertainty, etc. Simply and realistically, **pain is an unavoidable part of life**. Adversity and pain are as inevitable as night and day.

Also, join me in being reminded – **pain is as much a part of God's plan as pleasure**. I cannot count the times I avoided thanking Him for my gifts and moments of joy, yet, didn't hesitate to call Him out as a painful experience hit. **Thankfully, He is all-forgiving and chooses not to remember!**

I perceive life is less about thinking about dealing with pain and

more about how one reacts and handles the pain. Again, pain is real. There are times when a bit of whining and moaning felt pretty good as a method of releasing from the challenge and representative of my innate weakness as a human being.

Techniques I apply, when the most painful, physical moments hit are:

1. Pray Jesus place His healing hands upon me to release some of the pain.
2. Be conscience of my breathing – deeply, slowly in my nose and out of my mouth.
3. Play some soothing music while lying on the floor, couch or bed.
4. Take a hot shower or bath.
5. Sign up for a massage – the power of touch is an amazing Godsend!

Techniques in my handling emotional pain is more in-depth, addressed herein and will be explored in a future writing.

A spiritual statement that helps me better understand pain is:
Pain produces Perseverance,

Perseverance produces Perspective

while Perspective produces Hope!

Miracles ….. His Power

Nearly every time when being blessed with the opportunity to speak with church or civic groups and individuals, especially the devastating loss of Irene and my blessing of being able to walk when the prognosis said otherwise, listeners repeatedly call me a "living miracle". Many medical professionals also use this term when introducing me either to other patients or in a speech setting.

I am respectfully honored to be viewed in this regard. It is not my doing, but rather the power of our Almighty Father as He spared my life and continues to use me to reflect His power, understanding, forgiveness and master planning.

To me, watching our children continue to move forward with their lives, after facing a most horrific experience is much more miraculous than my journey. Each has taken the foundation Irene and I attempted to establish during their formative years and strengthen those works to build a bond of unbelievable strength and support for each other. With God's grace, Jen with Jason, Chris with Heather, and Janelle continue to move to new heights personally and professionally. Their ability to turn a loss of such magnitude into a motivational force for growth is our Lord's work and is therefore, to me, a miracle.

By being classified as a miracle, a situation defies medical or reasonable expectations based on a normal reaction or predictability. It is God's work that is a constant **MIRACLE**. Without

His hands upon me my accomplishments would not exist. I am without words to think God loves me enough to choose me to be an example of His work. The opportunity to see Irene crossover, is a miracle of miracles for me. Again, this experience is God's power, and the Holy Spirit continues to guide me in the manner to best share our circumstance with others. Following many of my initial speaking engagements, I would look back laughing as words came out of my mouth I didn't know were in my vocabulary. No doubt other experiences of the Holy Spirit are at work within me.

God is truly miraculous. I challenge every one of you to look back on your life and really think about how a certain situation could have turned out a little different if only ….. While lying in a hospital bed or rolling around in a wheelchair I had plenty of time to think about how often a spiritual hand took control of me when I was fluttering about. Turning myself over to God for Him to use me to do His work and realizing I am not in charge is a personal evolution that could have only occurred through the miracle of the Lord's patience, forgiveness and ultimate love for me.

Isn't the Bible itself a demonstration of a miracle to its highest degree? In existence for more than 2,000 years, written by 40 authors, across multiple continents, over a period of 1,500 years, this compilation withstood scrutiny of man's most accomplished scholars time and again.

Yet, the Bible remains a primary resource for answers that impact our world and contains the greatest story ever told – the resurrection of a man named Jesus who had been put to death three days prior for a purpose motivated by **LOVE** of men and women, an endless number of whom would live on this earth years after fulfilling His purpose.

The Bible contains a number of Jesus' works in miracle form as each reflects His awesome, limitless power. During my initial rehab, my reading of this great book led me to enjoy seeing our Lord's work in another miracle and heightened my belief that things were going to be better; **because of the existence of miracles EVERYTHING IS POSSIBLE!**

These days when speaking to patients, their family members and others facing life-changing challenges, each feels they cannot or will not survive, the Holy Spirit speaks through me to share assurance a miracle is right around the corner, regardless of the picture at hand. **It is important to understand that a miracle is always possible and available simply by connecting with God.** My method in accomplishing spiritual maturation leading to belief in miracles is outlined throughout this document. I encourage you, regardless of where you are today, to remain open to **reality of miracles** working – if not for you, for others in and around our world. **As each of us places a petition before God, He is pleased we turn to Him respecting and expecting His power.**

If you get one thing out of this book I pray **you are a special child of the Most High. Miracles can and will happen for you, regardless of your situation; nothing is too big or too challenging for Him to handle – and you will never know when God will do His work!**

I have learned any one of us should expect miracles and we can cause the happening of miracles. Miracles occur as a result of tremendous faith. Faith that is far above doubt as we are conditioned to the deepest faith possible as it releases the incredible power to miracles happen.

We become what we are in our thoughts. As we start to expect miracles, since God keeps all His promises, miracles happen. True faith raises any challenging circumstance above doubt and fear as it is God's promise to handle that which we cannot. Faith, a bright light is our world, is the opposite of doubt or darkness. As I continue to grow and practice faith by turning issues over to the Lord, a significant personality change for me, I feel remarkable power with peace. My perspective of life is new as I look toward the opportunities God has planned for me! Through my development of faith, deeper than I would have ever expected within my capability or worth, I continue to be blessed to face and conquer difficulties termed as impossible!

God created each of us with a built-in miracle principle. I am certain of this because God knows as human beings we often need to see in order to believe. When we witness a miracle our awareness of possibility is heightened. As we continue to grow in understanding God, we fertilize the possibility of miracles deep within our spiritual self to the point of expectation, looking for God to step in and provide an answer in the darkest of circumstance. In such a setting our Lord's power becomes apparent. That is why so often people have to experience their darkest situation or challenge to see the **light of His work.** Again, in referring to the Bible, there are numerous accounts of God stepping in when everything seemed hopeless. Have you heard of a guy called Job? If not, I encourage you to read his story while joining me in spiritual growth and understanding God's love in miracle form.

GOD SPECIALIZES IN THE IMPOSSIBLE!

Golf and Its Place .....

As a PGA (Professional Golfers' Association of America) member, I believe the game of golf is more than a game of a lifetime; my story tells you Golf is a Game of Life. The opportunities golf, as a game and as a business provided me, are blessings beyond comprehension. Qualities of a person earning the status of PGA Member equate to the highest quality of person in any vocation.

The organization has elevated the roll of golf player through stringent education and training to a high-qualified, diversified business manager. Every person connected to a club who has a PGA Professional on staff, in most cases the club's team leader, most generally enjoys a deeper appreciation for the wonderful game.

As a youngster, golf played a significant part of my life. Growing up caddying at Rutland Country Club in Vermont, real life education could not have had a better setting for me. The Head PGA Professional Henry Vergi, a true legend in the game, became more than a surrogate father for me. Mr. Vergi instilled lessons on how to act in a setting of the community's elite. Mr. Vergi said, "Always act like you've been here before." Those words stay with me to this day.

Many mornings Mr. Vergi would tell me to grab his bag as we headed off to the 10th tee. He played 3 or 4 balls and explained each shot before he played them. Few challenged Mr. Vergi's knowledge of the golf swing, especially his ability with a pitching wedge in hand. Walking between shots, I reaped extensive education as Mr. Vergi shared information about dealing with people and their challenges within the club setting. Mr. Vergi, the epitome of a PGA Professional and man, touched more young guys' lives in a positive way than he would ever know. When scheduled to give private golf lessons, Mr. Vergi permitted me to sit adjacent to him and his student, enabling me to hear instructions. Another PGA Professional that helped me understand aspects of the golf swing and the business of golf was Leo Reynolds. Although Leo lived miles away I met with him as often as I could. Today, Leo is still considered one of the finest golf teachers in the northeast. He too has touched an unlimited number of kids beyond golf and more in life.

The information I learned from both these classy guys remains invaluable as I developed my successful teaching philosophy for so many students throughout Vermont, Connecticut and the Carolinas. During rehabilitation, certain aspects of my teaching philosophy became very applicable, contributed to my walking and I believe they can be applied to other parts of our career and lives.

Use Clear, Positive Messages

The words we use, especially during our thinking and internal communication, are vital to the end result. Our mind interprets from positive words, which trigger physical reaction or motion. For instance, a golfer when putting tells himself – don't stop the stroke at the impact with the ball. His mind grabs the message

– stop at impact – and he does exactly what he told himself not to do. A more accomplished player would say – keep the stroke moving through impact toward the target line. This message is a clear, positive message.

During rehab, constantly applying positive words was vital. During every step I was consciously making sure my heel struck the ground first, rather than my toe. My message was clear – heel strike first. I avoided using the statement – don't let your toe hit the ground first. Inevitably, if I had, I would have stubbed my toe and tripped.

The world's most accomplished people, in golf and in life, work at eliminating negative words from their vocabulary and thought process. Each is a true expert at timely transition of negative, non-productive words replaced by positive action statements.

One's ability to convert negative words into positive is a learned behavior. The more we practice the sooner our mind sees and feels positive results, until we are to the point that a positive thought is first and foremost.

Visualization – Seeing the Result
Visualization is one's ability to develop a motion picture of an action or series of movements and seeing an end result.

A golf student is challenged to stand behind the ball, looking down their intended direction, seeing the ball in flight and landing next to the target.

While sitting in the wheelchair I closed my eyes, said a prayer, then saw myself taking a first step, then many. Visualizing my movement led way to my turning myself completely over to God and allowing His work to take hold, lead and support me.

Each waking moment, I committed myself to anything that improved my possibility to walk. Free time was filled with closed eyes, prayers, and reflecting on my pushing Janelle in a stroller and grocery cart. Often, I found myself in a trance of imagination to walking.

Visualization is an exercise utilized by accomplished people in all fields. Each sees themselves in performance and then the end result. Give it a shot and enjoy the results!

Staying in the Moment – Past v Present

The only reasonable aspect of my life I have control over is the present. I control my decision and effort at this time, the here and now. Once my action is taken or decision is made the results are in God's hands. Through **faith** I know His decision is best for me based on the plan He designed.

The past is gone while the future is ahead. The present is my opportunity to be all I can be and accomplish the best with complete focus.

As a golfer I cannot go back and replay a mis-hit shot or poorly played hole. Nor, as I stand on the 15th tee can I be effective playing that hole if I am concerned about my tee shot on the next hole. I can only focus on my game plan for the hole before executing shots based on my swing routine and practiced reaction.

My ability to concentrate, staying in the now, enhanced my ability to enjoy the process and then success. Inner strength, based primarily on a sense of peace, is attributed to a level of knowledge and preparation. So often we hear someone reflect on how much he or she enjoyed the process, doing their very best and accepted the result.

Where I've been is gone while where I'm headed is in His hands!

Paralysis by Analysis – Move out of Your own Way

Thinking is my opportunity to assess a situation with its relevance to me and the person or people that may be involved. Overthinking is, more often than not, a debilitating act which results in no action at all.

Many golfers have more natural ability than they believe. When using video swing analysis most often students say, "I don't look half bad swinging that club" as their confidence takes a sudden jump. We then proceed to the driving range as their initial shots are quite good. Shortly, though, an errant shot or two are struck as the student's personality makes a drastic change. It is clearly apparent, the mind is beginning to work as the motion becomes inconsistent. The natural motion becomes an action similar to a slow motion profile as one dissects a shot by thinking through nearly every aspect of the swing. Depending on the length of the swing, the motion is timed at between 3 and 7 seconds. In reality, how much real thinking can go on in that amount of time? We are more able to feel an aspect of a swing rather than think about it. More accomplished players practice an aspect of the swing, and through repetition, build a repetitive motion - referred to as muscle memory.

As I re-learned the motion of walking the same process took place. We often utilized a mirror so I could see my movement or lack thereof. Amber, Dr. Mike, or the therapist working with me, at the time, defined the physical movement until we agreed my understanding was clear. At that point I just attempted to do and allow my body to just do, minimizing thought to the point of elimination.

Each day we are confronted by circumstances that rarely are truly new. Based on experience and our natural feel our response is second nature. When I have found myself in a situation where over thought has kicked in, it has proven me better to stop, regroup, start over and go for it. Few accomplished people extend beyond their natural response time when making the vast majority of their decisions.

Decision-making leading to success is the result of inner peace or confidence, the strength of conviction by doing right.

Forward Thinking – Dealing with the Past

The words of direction or encouragement, "just forget about it and move on" are much easier said than done. Each time I returned to the past I placed myself in the position of being a victim instead of developing the courage to move on. The past causes procrastination and works against me by delaying and enjoying a healthy future.

Negative experiences are the challenge to make me stronger and more determined if I decide to believe. My ability to be able to move on is directly related to my ability to release the past and remain focused on the next step.

The game of golf provides a perfect example of people allowing a previous state of mind to control their result. Golfers play within a comfort zone, as the most accomplished continue to challenge themselves, through quality instruction and practice, to learn shots that are new to them until proficient.

One's ability to keep the past in perspective is the foundation for moving forward. Our mind remains in constant motion by thought. Few aspects of our world are stationary or motionless. **Life is moving. It is seldom if ever motionless!**

Consider repeating the following statement throughout your day:
- I know I can have whatever I am ready and willing to receive.
- I accept my past is gone; it can't be changed.
- I forgive my mistakes – I know mistakes are human and I will work to avoid repeating the same mistake.

- I will keep my thoughts in the present, should I slip back in the past.
- I know the past will drift away, as I let it go.

Life's Fulfillment – Balance

Before you close your eyes at night, how do you evaluate the success of your day? Is your day based on the amount of money you made or saved? In your eyes is your day successful because you closed the big deal or finally completed a particular task? Perhaps you jumped on the scale and saw a loss of 2 pounds? Is seeing an accomplishment of your son or daughter the device by which you measure your day? Perhaps you are on the team that won the Super Bowl? Clearly, success is measured through different eyes in different ways.

Following the shattering of my life, I really started to look at my personal definition of being successful. Throughout my exploration time a statement Irene would often make to me made more and more sense.

In terms of being a country club manager and golf professional my success was apparent. The club was doing well and my goal of being an all-around qualified, respected manager seemed realized. Heck, nearly every morning I was at the club by 6 or 6:30 am and worked until 8 or 9 pm, unless there was event which kept me there until 1 or 2 am. By my standard, I was "the man" and was working my butt off to stay there. Oh, yes, this was my schedule at least 6 days a week. On the 7th day, more often than not, I at least had to be there to see the place open. The club certainly could not operate unless I was there to get it going. **So I thought I was successful!**

Back to Irene's statement – "Reggie, you are entitled to a life. You have a family. We have worked hard to have, yet, when do we enjoy?" Granted, our lifestyle was good and our children had what they wanted. On the days I did dare to leave at 6 or 7 pm, usually prompted by Irene's "request", we would enjoy a dinner out and a bit of "us" time. Occasionally, in the morning she would suggest, "Why don't you call in and at least spend the morning with me?" From time to time I did, but many of those times Irene would suggest I just go to the club as that was where my head appeared to be. A week's vacation most often started the first couple of days with my focus still on club issues.

In looking back, I was present for our kids' school and personal activities. Needless to say, my presence was a result of a loving wife and mother's persistent phone calls. Her patience was obviously immeasurable.

When I realized my presence in this world, following the accident, my initial prayers were driven by a request for **forgiveness from Irene**, for all the time I had taken from her by not being with her.

I was taught a most painful life lesson – **you don't know what you have until you no longer have it!** The level of my selfishness took me a long time to forgive.

One of my biggest sins was my lack of honoring our God by caring for all that is His — my wife, our children and myself, in a complete manner. I thought because I was providing a good life for my family I was being honorable and in His graces. As I grew in my understanding of God's word, I realized how wrong I was.

God expects a balanced life - too much of anything is dishonoring!
As a golf instructor, I stressed balance was from start to finish of a swing. All athletic actions require balance to enhance success. As a club manager, developing and applying a balanced operations program enhances effectiveness. Business plans are designed aimed at balance to develop a positive bottom line. As a manager of people balancing my time within each area of the operation was productive. Aspects of effective personnel management is availability and honesty.

Successful people in all vocations write, speak and function under fundamental practices, concentrating on balance and consistency. This focus wasn't a new-found, secret approach that only the most accomplished applied — balance was outlined in The Bible, the longest standing training document ever prepared. It is stressed within our personal selves, families, churches and communities.

There are **four (4) primary aspects** of life that require **balanced** attention:

Spiritual   One's whole being comes from God's plan. A primary purpose of life is to honor Him by doing His will. More than just the weekly hour or two of attending service, daily living is predicated to that which God commands. In the three other aspects of my life, the Bible outlines direction for each of us to honor the Lord through family, vocation and personal actions.

Family   The Bible clearly directs a husband to honor his wife – to love and cherish her as the precious wedding vows state. Words about loving, providing for and protecting for one's family are also said. A father teaches his children by example, about aspects of life, including the importance of maintaining a balanced approach to daily living. A truly successful relationship between spouses reflects both individual's ability and willingness to balance giving and taking.

Vocational   Work is an important means to today's life. During these challenging economic times pressure in this area of life may require a little extra, but through constant prayer and quality family time the institution of family will be stronger than ever. Words in The Bible
direct work be done in an honoring manner to Him. Does a successful home life not make work easier and vice versa?

Self   We are each an instrument of God's love. He created us with purpose in a designed plan. It is up to us to connect with the Lord to learn that purpose and fulfill it. As God's property, satan constantly tempts us to throw ourselves out of balance, just like the misleading of Eve and Adam. As we stay committed to living by "doing right"- guidance we have through the presence of the

Holy Spirit in that little voice deep inside, our purpose will take its shape. The purpose can only be assured because He designed it – and balanced steps will lead us to the top of a mountain we may have never expected! As I took my "*2nd First Steps*", I knew He was there to hold me up and catch me if I began to fall.

And moving on with my blessed life …..

After nearly one year from the day of the accident, I returned to work on a full-time basis with The Country Club of the Crystal Coast in Pine Knoll Shores. Club members; Phil, Jean, John Macheca and Everette Edwards, employees; Lorraine and Andy Ipock and I were talking as we noted the irony of the club situation. Just prior to the accident the club's Board of Directors entered into a contract to construct a new clubhouse, which was well underway. Our administration and pro shop operations were located in on-site temporary buildings. As the temps were being set in place we discussed location of a handicap access. Little did we know the need for the ramps was going to be for the club manager as I returned to work in a wheelchair. Who would have ever thought that on the weekend of April 15 of the previous year, a weekend trip would turn out being such a life-changing event?

I continued outpatient therapy with Deena, Roxanne and the other valuable members of the rehab team at Carolina Therapy, the same group that worked with me prior to my admittance to New Hanover Medical Center. When I first returned home, much of my time was spent in a wheelchair and with an occasional walker.

Within a couple months, my recovery progressed to eliminate the wheelchair to the walker, a pronged cane to a straight cane. Athletic trainer Paul Gilliken with the Sports Center Athletic Club in Morehead City, was instrumental in designing a strength/flexible enhancement program which also helped so much.

Just a few months later, Jennifer became a staff member as our membership activities coordinator and later the food & beverage area team leader. During the remainder of 2007, in addition to my responsibilities of overseeing normal club operations, we were also challenged to complete the clubhouse and new swimming pool construction projects, purchase all furnishings and equipment as well as developing the final overall operating plans for the facilities once opened. I believe this volume of work helped me adjust to life without my wife by keeping me busy. Going home each day, though, was still so extremely difficult.

On a personal note, Chris and Heather were busy finalizing plans for their upcoming August 11th wedding, and it was exciting to have Heather formally become part of the Colomb family. It is also important I mention Heather's parents, Bim and Becky Staton, who had been so supportive to our family. Their presence was extremely meaningful as Bim had been in a life battle of his own - a personal battle with cancer that began more than a couple years before our accident. Still, the couple was consistently positive, upbeat and loving.

Later the same year Jen announced her engagement to Jason Salter. During my return home, Jason was tremendously helpful, which enabled Chris to return to school at UNC-Wilmington. UNCW is a school that also had been so supportive to Chris and our family. During the final writing stages of this book I could be found at the UNCW library feeling very comfortable and blessed for the roll the school played in our family's journey.

In early summer of 2008, the new clubhouse was successfully opened. Just a month before, Jen worked to become a nationally certified wedding planner. The beautiful setting became one of the area's primary locations to have a wedding reception, private party, business meeting or golf event.

Jen and Jason were married on September 26th in a lovely ceremony. It was great to add Jason as another son!

Throughout the year the need for physical therapy was reduced while my continued improvement occurred with focus on weight lifting, flexibility and balance improvement exercises. My relationship with Dr. Stephen Greer of North River Prime Care continued while he referred me to Dr. Susan Vettichira, a long-term pain management specialist. Mark Stevens replaced Dr. Greer and continues to tend to my medical needs.

During the spring of 2009 I began experiencing increased pain in my back and ribs. Dr. Vettichira ran tests and recognized my continued work habits were detrimentally placing increased stress on my damaged frame. In her very caring, professional demeanor, Dr. Vettichira stated "Reggie, if you continue to work at the pace you are then you will be in that wheelchair that you were so determined to stay out of." She then implied I have another calling. Effectively managing a country club is extremely demanding, especially as one also performs the duties of a club's head golf professional. My average work week averaged between 60 and 70 hours. Dr. Vettichira's words repeated those I so often heard from Irene, "A job is part of your life. It is not your life."

I spoke with Club President Jean Turner as we came to an agreement, I would retire August 1st and move forward with needed surgery and further recovery.

Later in June, Janelle was recognized as West Carteret High School graduating Valedictorian. This was another tremendously proud moment for our whole family as Janelle told me, "Daddy, when mommy died I made a promise to her that I would be the Valedictorian. I worked so hard for this and am proud. I know she was watching over me during my speech." Her words were appreciated by a full gymnasium and an overflow room of people; many who approached Janelle at the end of the event with their eyes filled with tears.

In October I went to Portland to meet with Dr. John Mayberry and RN Ellen Peck with The Oregon Science and Health University, for evaluation. Interestingly, Joel and Victoria Osteen were in Portland that evening to speak. Frantically, I tried to purchase a ticket, since the program was sold out. By God's blessing I was able to purchase one outside the gathering and enjoyed the Lord's message of fortitude and commitment through the Osteens. The next day I again met with Dr. Mayberry and he agreed to operate on me, but said he would not be able to tell me the extent of my required surgery until he had opened me up. The surgery was scheduled for three weeks later. Jen accompanied me for the operation. I returned home to recouperate until the first part of 2010. I cannot thank Jason enough for his constant assistance upon my return to Morehead.

Since that time I committed to deepen spiritual awareness, my personal therapy and pursuit of deeper understanding of family dynamics especially when confronted by life's challenges, their successes and shortcomings. Most rewarding has been numerous opportunities for God to utilize me to share my experiences and His word to so many hospitalized and recovering patients along with their family members, as well as church, civic and medical related staffs.

Writing this book has motivated me to deeper understand experiences contained herein and look forward to further interaction with people I am blessed to meet in the future. God has also called me to life coaching, especially with people confronted by seriously challenging conditions. I also recently completed certification as a Grief Recovery Application Specialist, a topic I have found to be applicable to so many life situations from loss of employment and divorce, to the passing of a loved one. Grief is often stored within us from very early in our life. Its often debilitating effects may continue to compound themselves, sometimes deep inside of us until we face the challenges of facing its harsh realities and impact. This topic will be further explored in future writings.

Also, since spending over thirty years as a PGA Golf Professional, now a Life Member, I look forward to completing a golf instruction manual. Through the game of golf, I learned many life skills, and the PGA is a brotherhood, and sisterhood, made up of many fine people God has brought into this world to touch people's lives in an endless number of ways, beyond a game called Golf. To PGA Professionals – Golf is more than a game – it is a game that challenges the inner self of everyone who ever attempts to strike a golf shot.

The instruction manual will reflect my teaching philosophy I have shared with so many people utilizing an easy-to-understand approach to fundamentals while applying analogies of our daily lives.

With respect to Jen, Chris and Janelle - I am so proud of each of them as each moves forward with their lives.

Jennifer and her husband, Jason have a beautiful daughter, Ashlynd and live in Morehead City, NC. Jen recently received her MBA in Gerontology Administration with the UNC-Wilmington and is employed as a care facility assistant administrator while Jason, employed with a wine distributing company, completed a Business Administration Degree with Carteret Community College. He is pursuing the coveted status of Certified Specialist of Wine, as well.

Christopher and his wife, Heather, are enjoying their first home in Charlotte, NC. Chris is a Certified Public Account and is finalizing his Certified Financial Planner status. Heather is a licensed clinical therapist practicing in the Charlotte area. Both Chris and Heather received their MBA and MSW, respectively, from UNCW, as well. Unfortunately, in 2008, Heather's dad, Bim, passed away following his lengthy, courageous battle against cancer. Surely, he is surely enjoying eternity with Irene. Her mom, Becky, a teacher will be retiring in the near future.

Janelle graduated from West Carteret High School in Morehead City. As previously stated, she was recognized as the school's Valedictorian. Her touching graduation speech contained reflection of a person who had lived a whole life at such a tender age. Its depth so eloquently reminded listeners to enjoy the unlimited number of gifts we wake to each day.

Janelle is a student at Cornell University School of Engineering, in Ithaca, New York.

As with our other children, Janelle's display of inner fortitude may be the most powerful reflection of the strength of **family love**.

These days I am so blessed to enjoy watching my first grandchild as she grows. Spending time with her mom and dad, Chris, Heather and Janelle, as they face additional life challenges with such strong conviction, constantly reminds me of God's blessings and the impact Irene has made with each of these special people along with the other precious people that remain part of my life today!

Notes/Comments

Special Recognition…..

….. for the precious words contained in

New King James Bible

published by:

Tyndale House Publishers, Inc. 1979

Author .....

Reginald (Reggie) Colomb, is a native of Rutland, Vermont. There he met and married Irene Ann Godzik. The couple had three children – Jennifer, Christopher and Janelle. Unexpectedly, their family experienced a tragedy that would change each individual forever.

Reggie is a life member of the Professional Golfers' Association of America (PGA) and was a member of the Club Managers' of America (CMA) during his thirty plus years as a club manager and golf professional. He enjoyed an accomplished professional and amateur golfing career which included, during his enlistment, participation as a member of the United States Air Force golf team training camps. Also, Reggie is recognized as a premiere golf teacher throughout New England, North and South Carolinas. He managed the following clubs: Manchester C.C., Vt., Roxboro C.C., N.C., Mid Carolina Club, Prosperity, S.C. and The C.C. of the Crystal Coast, Carteret County, N.C. Reggie was also co-owner of New England Discount Golf, Rutland, Vt. and teaching instructor with Prospect Bay Country Club on Lake Bomoseen, Vt. Throughout his club management career Reggie also consulted with other clubs in Vermont and the Carolinas. His PGA Apprenticeship was served with Brooklawn Country Club, Fairfield, Ct. and Burlington Country Club, Vt.

In August 2009, Reggie was led to a new vocation – spending time with medical patients and their families, medical staffs as well as church and civic groups – sharing his inspirational story of courage and personal growth. He has formed, *"RMCLifePub"*, which is a Life Coaching Program to share messages to precious people challenged with life-changing events. With a solid foundation based on real life experience – including physical, emotional and spiritual treatment and extensive research to reinforce these areas of individual and family life. Reggie is also a Certified Grief Recovery Specialist. His positive, upbeat approach is committed to touch an endless number of lives.

Need
additional
copies?

To order more copies of

Second 1ˢᵗ Step .....

contact NewBookPublishing.com

❐   Order online at

NewBookPublishing.com/Bookstore

❐   Call 877-311-5100 or

❐   Email Info@NewBookPublishing.com

Call for multiple copy discounts!

 **Reliance
Media**